2-23-25

# COLLEGEBOUND REVIEW PSAT® & SAT® EXAMS STRATEGY GUIDE

*includes*
*Accepted: College Planning Strategies*
*for High School Families*

# COLLEGEBOUND REVIEW SIGNATURE PSAT® & SAT® EXAMS STRATEGY GUIDE

## STRUCTURE OF THE PSAT® AND SAT® EXAMS

Both the PSAT® and the SAT® consist of two hours and fourteen minutes of testing material and are comprised of four sections referred to as "modules."

## READING AND WRITING: Modules 1 and 2  (32 minutes each)

Modules 1 and 2, each with 27 questions, comprise the Reading and Writing Test.  The modules are composed of one paragraph stories, each followed by one question. The beginning portion of the module focuses on reading comprehension questions, while the latter portion focuses on grammatical and punctuation questions. The 27 paragraphs, and the single question that follows each one, address a multitude of subjects studied by high school students including literature, history, social studies, the humanities, and science.  All questions are multiple choice (A through D), and are based on information presented in the passage as students are not expected to recall specific facts learned over the years. With 32 minutes for each module, students have just over one minute to answer each question.

The passages range between 25 and 150 words in length and vary greatly in levels of complexity. Some are based on the reading and analytical skills expected of middle school students, while others test the skills expected of college freshmen.

All students taking the PSAT® or SAT® have an identical Module 1, considered to be of average difficulty. Depending on how well a student performs on Module 1, he/she will move onto either an easier, or a more difficult, Module 2. This is referred to as "two-stage adaptive testing." Test-takers who perform well on Module 1 are given harder questions on Module 2 "to determine the upper limits of their skills and knowledge," according to College Board. Those who don't perform as well on Module 1 get easier questions on Module 2. Of course, this ultimately impacts one's final score.

## Math: Modules 1 and 2  (35 minutes each)

Modules 1 and 2, each with 22 questions, comprise the Math test. The Math questions on the PSAT® and SAT® cover Algebra, Geometry, Trigonometry, Advanced Math, and Problem-Solving & Data Analysis. There are no Pre-Calculus or Calculus questions on these exams.

With 22 questions to answer on each Module, within a time frame of 35 minutes, students have about 1.5 minutes to solve each problem.  About 75% of the questions are multiple choice in format, with options of A through D. The remainder use the "student-produced response" format, whereby students must come up with their own answer and bubble it in following specific rules.

Algebra and Advanced Math comprise the majority of the Math test, with 13 to 15 questions on each of these two areas (totaling 70% of test questions). The Algebra questions test students' understanding of linear relationships, while the Advanced Math questions test students' understanding of non-linear relationships.

There are also 5 to 7 questions (about 15%) focused on Problem-Solving & Data Analysis, including problems with percentages, ratios, one and two variable data, probability, and scatterplots. Likewise, Geometry and Trigonometry also contribute 5 to 7 questions, including area, volume, lines, angles, triangles, and circles. The Trigonometry question(s) typically deal with right triangles (sin x = cos y) and SOHCAHTOA.

The Math test is also adaptive, with Module 2 questions based on a student's success on the Module 1 questions. Use of a calculator is allowed on both Math modules. Students can use the online calculator or one that they bring with them. Cell phones, of course, cannot be used as calculators.

# Reading and Writing Modules
## Collegebound Review
## Signature Strategies

1. **Know what to expect**. The first Reading & Writing module will have an assortment of questions with mixed levels of complexity, while the second module will be either more or less difficult, depending on your accuracy on the first module. Approximately 29 of the questions will focus on critical reading skills and about 25 of the questions will focus on writing skills (punctuation, grammar, word choice, and sentence structure).

2. **First, read the question located at the end of the story**. Each story is only one paragraph long, so it's easiest to read the question, prior to reading the paragraph, to determine what you are looking for. Some typical questions are:

   *Which choice completes the text with the most logical and precise word or phrase?*

   *Which choice best states the main purpose of the text?*

3. **Take your time**. You will have about 70 seconds (more than a minute!), on average, to answer each question. So, after reading the question, read each "story" once, carefully, at whatever speed works for you, and then answer the question that follows. Do practice tests under timed conditions in advance to ensure that your natural pace will allow you to finish the module on time. Extra time, upon completion of the module, is not useful. So, it's best to determine your pacing in advance.

4. **Answer each question as you work your way through the module**. There is no penalty for wrong answers, so it's important to answer each question. If you don't have a "favorite" answer, use the *answer elimination* tool to narrow down your options and then take your best guess. Do not make random guesses, and do not skip questions with the intention of going back to them later. You likely won't have time to re-read the paragraph and carefully reconsider the answer, and it won't be any easier the second time around.

5. **Concentrate on what the paragraph is saying**. This is known as *active reading*. When students read a paragraph while thinking about how bored they are, or where they'd rather be, the results are underwhelming. It's vital to focus on what the author is saying and then seek the answer to the previously read question that appears at the end of the paragraph. Realize that you will be spending about 70 seconds on each story. Colleges certainly expect applicants to have an attention span that will allow them to stay focused for at least that length of time.

6. **When working on Writing questions, read the paragraph aloud in your mind.** The writing questions focus on proper grammar and punctuation. While you can't talk aloud, by "hearing" the sentences in your head, you will frequently know which answer choice sounds correct.

Questions often focus on parallel sentence structure, use of the proper tense, correct word choice (vocabulary), and proper use of punctuation signs.

7. **Carefully consider "word choice" questions**. When answering questions that ask you to complete the text with the *most logical and precise word or phrase*, think of a word you would use to "fill in the blank," and then choose the word from the options offered that is closest in meaning and works in the context of the sentence. Consider, for example, a sentence that states, "Fear of an approaching hurricane forced the family to _____ their home." You need a word that means "to leave," within the proper context. *Depart, vacate, retire,* and *evacuate* all mean "to leave," but only *evacuate* works in the context of the sentence.

8. **Review the proper use of punctuation signs**. Many questions will test you on the proper usage of the comma, semicolon, and colon, so go into the test confident of the rules for each one.

## Comma

For a quick review, remember that a comma separates a word, or group of words, in a sentence. I find it helpful to read the sentence, aloud, in my mind. At any spot where I would pause, I insert a comma. When there are two commas in a sentence, it should make sense if you read it while leaving out the words between the commas.

e.g. Professor Theodore Smith, chairman of the Economics Department at Duke University, won a Nobel Prize.

## Semicolon

A strategy for the use of a semicolon is to check if it separates two phrases that could each stand alone as a grammatically correct sentence. When a semicolon is used correctly, you should be able to replace it with a period and capitalize the following word.

e.g. I love drinking coffee first thing each morning; my best friend prefers green tea.

## Colon

A colon is most frequently used when followed by a list. But be sure not to put a colon after the words "such as" or "including." At these times, separate each listing with a comma.

e.g. I went to Staples to buy office supplies: three desks, six chairs, and two bookcases.

I went to Staples to buy office supplies, including three desks, six chairs, and two bookcases.

9. **Take note of transition questions**, asking which word or phrase best connects two sentences. Below is a typical question:

*The Lions basketball team expected to lose the championship game to their more experienced competitor, the Bears. _____, they were shocked when they won the tournament.*

*Which choice completes the text with the most logical transition?*

A) But
B) Similarly
C) Thus
D) For example

The correct answer is "thus" which means "therefore" or "as a result or consequence of this."

10. **Be aware that the writing style favored on this test is that of a journalist**. When asked to choose the best way to re-word a sentence, the correct answer is almost always the shortest answer. Be succinct, concise, to the point. And never choose an answer that is redundant (saying the same thing twice) within the context of a sentence. Examples: "repeat again," "it happened annually each year," "the audience's response was tremendous, even overwhelming."

# Math Modules
# Collegebound Review
# Signature Strategies

1. **Work at a comfortable pace.** Each of the two Math modules has 22 questions to be completed within a time frame of 35 minutes, allowing an average time of just over 1.5 minutes per question. Work at a diligent pace, but not so quickly that accuracy is sacrificed. Do practice tests in advance to feel comfortable with the pacing required to answer all the questions within the provided time frame. Focus first on the questions you are easily able to solve and then use the remaining time to deal with the more difficult questions, ultimately guessing if necessary.

2. **Use scrap paper that is provided**, making each question as visual as possible. Work through each problem, step by step, on paper and then use your calculator to find the solution.

3. **Narrow down your potential answers**, when struggling with a question. Then back into the correct answer. For example, if asked to identify the slope of a graph, the question will typically give two answer choices with a positive slope and two answer choices with a negative slope. Most students, by simply looking at the pictured graph, can identify whether the line is moving up (positive slope) or down (negative slope) as it goes from left to right. This will narrow down the potentially correct answer to two choices, making it easier to solve. At this point, even random guessing will provide a 50% chance of earning credit.

4. **Know the proper way to record your answers**. Most of the questions are multiple choice, but some of the math questions ask students to record the answer rather than select it from options A through D. It's important for students to know, ahead of time, the proper way to record their answers so they do not waste valuable time deciphering the directions. Rules for recording answers are as follows:

- If you find more than one correct answer, record only one answer.

- Your answer can be up to 5 characters for a positive answer and up to 6 characters (including the negative sign) for a negative answer.

- If your answer is a fraction that is too long (over 5 characters for positive, 6 characters for negative), write the decimal equivalent.

- If your answer is a decimal that is too long (over 5 characters for positive, 6 characters for negative), truncate it or round at the fourth digit.

- If your answer is a mixed number (such as three-and-a-half), write it as an improper fraction (7/2) or as its decimal equivalent (3.5).

- Don't include symbols such as a percent sign, comma, or dollar sign in your answer.

- On all questions, there's no penalty for wrong answers so it's important to answer every question, even if it's a guess. There is a countdown clock and calculator built into the program, but you can still bring a watch and calculator if you desire. (It's a good idea to do so!)

5. **Read each question carefully**, paying attention to the details. Below is a typical question. To solve, you need to divide 120 by 60 to change seconds to minutes.

   *If a secretary can type at an average rate of 120 words per minute, how many words, on average, can the secretary type per second?*

   The correct answer is 2

   Often, when a question provides two equations, the solution is obtained by adding the two equations together or subtracting one equation from the other. In the following sample question, students need to add the two equations to get 2y = 36.

   *6x = 24      -6x + 2y = 12*

   *The solution to the given system of equations is (x, y). What is the value of y?*

   The correct answer is 18

6. **Utilize tools provided.** There is a formula box at the beginning of each Math module, so refer to it when needed for geometric formulas. It will provide the following information:

- Area of a circle = $\pi r^2$

- Circumference of a circle = $2\pi r$

- Area of a rectangle = length • width

- Area of a triangle = $1/2$ • base • height

- Pythagorean theorem: $c^2 = a^2 + b^2$

- The proportion of side measurements of a 30 – 60 – 90 degree right triangle is, respectively: $x$, $x\sqrt{3}$, $2x$

- The proportion of side measurements of a 45 – 45 – 90 degree right triangle is, respectively: s, s, $s\sqrt{2}$

- Volume of a rectangular solid = length • width • height

- Volume of a cylindrical solid = $\pi r^2$ • height

- Volume of a sphere = $4/3\pi r^3$

- Volume of a cone = $1/3\pi r^2$ • height

- Volume of a pyramid = $1/3$ • length • width • height

- The number of degrees of arc in a circle is 360.

- The number of radians of arc in a circle is $2\pi$

- The sum of the measures in degrees of the angles of a triangle is 180.

7. **Memorize two formulas that are not provided in the formula box**. Students are often tested on the center-radius form of the circle equation: $(x-h)^2 + (y-k)^2 = r^2$ with the center at (h, k) and r = radius. They are also tested on the quadratic formulas: $ax^2 + bx + c = 0$ and $x = \dfrac{-b \pm \sqrt{b^2 - 4ac}}{2a}$

A sample question provided by College Board requiring use of the center-radius form of the circle equation is as follows:

*A circle in the xy-plane has a diameter with endpoints (4,10) and (4,16). An equation of this circle is $(x-2)^2 + (y-9)^2 = r^2$, where r is a positive constant. What is the value of $r^2$?*

*As the Y values of the endpoints are 10 and 16, that is a distance of 6, so the diameter equals 6.*

*Radius is half of the diameter, so the radius equals 3.*

*Question: What is the value of $r^2$?*

$3^2 = 9$

The correct answer is 9

A sample question requiring use of the quadratic formula, is as follows: $-9x^2 + 30x + c = 0$

**In the given equation, c is a constant. The equation has exactly one solution. What is the value of c?**

According to the quadratic formula, $ax^2 + bx + c = 0$

In this equation, a=-9, b=30, and we need to solve for c.

Discriminant is $b^2 - 4ac$
$30^2 - 4(-9)c = 0$
$900 + 36c = 0$
$900 = -36c$
$C = -25$

The correct answer is -25

8. **Bring a calculator** if you feel it is easier to use than the one built into the digital exam and utilize provided scrap paper to draw diagrams and help visualize test questions.

9. **Familiarize yourself with the Math that is covered on the PSAT® & SAT® exams.** All the questions are based on

material learned in Algebra I, Geometry, and Algebra II. There is no Pre-Calculus or Calculus on the exam, so students currently in advanced Math classes often need to review concepts learned in previous years.

The topics most frequently addressed are as follows:

- Order of Operations
- Substitution & Elimination to Solve a System of Equations
- Fractions
- Inequalities
- Absolute Value
- Linear Relationships
- Interpreting Functions
- Percentages
- Ratios, Proportions, and Direct and Inverse Variation Rules
- Mean, Median, Mode, and Range
- Probability and Statistics
- Factoring
- Advanced Equation Concepts
- Synthetic Division
- Function Notation & Manipulation
- Exponents
- Zeros and Parabolas
- Trigonometry
- Circles and Triangles

**For further practice on both the Reading/Writing and Math modules, utilize official sample tests in *The Official Digital SAT Study Guide* and on the Bluebook computer/tablet digital testing application by College Board.**

# Test Strategies for All Modules

- **Answer Every Question**

There is no penalty for guessing on the PSAT® or SAT®, so be sure to record an answer for every question. Even on the Math grid-in questions, which have many more potential answers than the multiple choice questions, put down a number so you have at least a chance of earning credit.

- **Focus on Understanding the Question**

Make sure you know exactly what you are being asked. If it's a Math problem, are you being asked to solve for x, or 2x, or x - 5? On multiple choice questions, the correct answer is one option, but "distractor answers" (which you will get if you make a careless mistake) are often the other options.

- **Come Back to Questions If Needed**

On Math questions, "flag" any question that you don't know how to do or that will take you a great deal of time. You want to get the greatest number of questions correct, so flag any particularly difficult questions, move on, and then return later – even if only to guess.

- **Use Your Scrap Paper**

This is particularly helpful for Math questions, allowing you to draw diagrams, work through equations, solve problems step-by-step, and simplify and visualize each problem.

- **Make Full Use of Allotted Time**

There is no advantage to completing a module with time to spare, so do practice tests under timed conditions in advance to figure out your pacing. You want to work through each question carefully and methodically, while having time to complete each module.

- **Do Not Look for "Trick Questions"**

For each question, there is one definitive answer. There are not trick questions. Before inclusion on an SAT®, each question is pre-tested on hundreds of students to be sure that it performs as expected. Each question is also reviewed by test developers and educators. So do not second-guess yourself; mark the answer that you think is accurate. If unsure, use the *answer elimination* tool to narrow down your options and then take your best guess.

- **Familiarize Yourself With Test Directions**

By referring to practice tests, ahead of time, in "The Official Digital SAT Study Guide," students can go into their SAT® knowing the directions for each test section. Then, valuable testing time will not be consumed by reading directions. The directions on the actual tests will be exactly the same, word for word, as the directions in the Study Guide. Having a firm grasp of the directions is particularly helpful on the Math modules, where there are detailed instructions on answering the student-produced response questions.

- **Proper Preparation**

The Bluebook digital testing application offers multiple full length, adaptive, and scored SAT® practice test exams. Bluebook can be downloaded on a Windows laptop or tablet, an Apple laptop, or an iPad, on College Board's website. There are also full-length linear sample tests offered on their website for additional practice. Practice tests are most effective in raising exam scores when students fully understand the correct answer breakdown for all questions they answered incorrectly. This instruction is offered at all Collegebound Review PSAT/SAT® preparation classes and private one-on-one strategy lessons with step-by-step answer demonstrations provided on a whiteboard.

# Protocols to Prepare for the Digital Exams

## In advance of your SAT® test day:

- Utilizing the device you will use on test day, download the Bluebook exam application on College Board's website. Your device should be either a personal or school-managed Windows laptop or tablet, personal or school-managed Mac laptop or iPad, or school-managed Chromebook.

- After signing into Bluebook, read and accept the application *Terms and Conditions*.

- Go to *Practice and Prepare* on the homepage to try some sample SAT® questions in the test preview or take a full-length digital SAT® practice test. You can then review your test results and identify where you need to improve.

- Five days before your test day, go to the Bluebook homepage and find your SAT® under *Your Tests*. Complete the short exam set-up and get your admission ticket. You can take a picture of your admission ticket, print it, or email it to yourself. If you need to make any changes to your admission ticket, you can update it until three days before your test by contacting customer service at College Board.

- You need to bring an acceptable photo ID to your test site. Review College Board's ID requirements in advance.

- It's important for students to know, ahead of time, the proper way to record their answers so they do not waste valuable time deciphering the directions. Most of the questions are multiple choice, though some of the Math questions ask students to record their answer rather than select it from options A through D.

**On your SAT® test day, bring the following items:**

- Admission ticket. You can use your cell phone to show your admission ticket, but your phone will be collected before the test begins.

- Acceptable photo ID.

- Computer, with Bluebook application already downloaded, and its power cable. There is no guarantee that you will have access to an outlet, so your device should be fully charged and able to last for 3 hours.

- Pens or pencils for scratch work. Do not bring scrap paper as it will be provided.

- An acceptable calculator for use on the Math section if you prefer using a handheld calculator to the embedded calculator in Bluebook. Review College Board's list of acceptable calculators.

- An external mouse, if you use one.

- An external keyboard if you use one. (External keyboards can only be used with tablets, not with laptops.)

## On your SAT® test day, do NOT bring:

- Smartwatches, wearable technology such as fitness trackers, or detachable privacy screens as they will be collected and held during testing.

- Bluetooth devices such as wireless earbuds or headphones.

- Other prohibited items listed by College Board

## Arrive on time:

- Plan to arrive earlier than the time indicated on your admission ticket. Doors typically close at 8:00 a.m., unless otherwise noted. You will not be admitted after this time.

- If you are approved to borrow a testing device from College Board, arrive by 7:15 a.m. to pick up your device, sign into Bluebook, and set up your test.

## Testing Typically Starts Between 8:15 and 8:45 a.m.

- You will be assigned a seat by your proctor.

- You'll then log into the center's Wi-Fi and open the Bluebook application, which will guide you through instructions.

- The proctor can answer questions only about procedure, not about test questions or content.

- The proctor will give you a start code. Once you enter the start code, testing will begin, and Bluebook will keep track of the time you have remaining in each test section.

- Each student is timed individually so you'll take breaks and complete testing at slightly different times.

- Each section of the test (Reading/Writing and Math) has two parts called modules, and each module is timed separately.

- You can move back and forth between questions in a module and review your answers until time expires.

- Once you've moved on from a module, you cannot go back to it.

- When the test is over, your answers are submitted automatically. If your submission fails, for any reason, you'll have the opportunity to resubmit as your answers will be saved to your device.

**During the test, you'll have access to a set of tools:**

- On both Math modules, you'll find a reference sheet (with Geometry formulas) as well as a built-in graphing calculator. You are also allowed to bring your own calculator.

- On Reading and Writing questions, use the annotation tool to highlight text or leave yourself a note, if you so choose.

- If you are struggling with a multiple-choice question, use the *answer elimination* tool to narrow down your options and then back into the correct answer.

- A zoom feature allows you to read graphics and reading material more easily.

- A built-in clock allows you to see how much time remains on your testing module.

- You can "flag" any questions you want to come back to later. This is helpful on the Math modules.

- If you have a problem during the test, raise your hand to ask the proctor for help or click the Help icon for troubleshooting tips.

**Breaks:**

- Students will have one 10-minute break, between the Reading/Writing and the Math modules. You can take an unscheduled break if you need to, but you'll lose testing time.

- When taking a break, leave your device open; **don't** close your device.

- Keep your ID with you at all times as it will be checked every time you enter the testing room.

- If you brought a calculator, it must remain on your desk during breaks.

# Scoring the SAT®

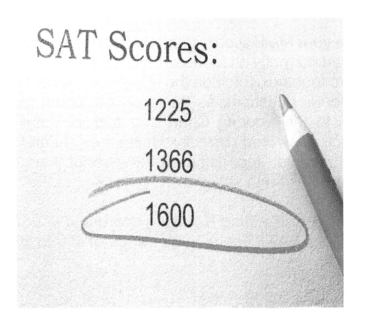

The PSAT® is scored on a range of 160 to 760 points in each of two areas, with a combined score in the range of 320 to 1520 total points. A PSAT® selection index score (48-228) for possible National Merit® Scholarship Program entry is also provided. The score portal allows students to compare their total score to the average scores of all test takers from their school, state, and country on that particular exam date.

The SAT® is scored on a range of 200 to 800 points in each of two areas, with a combined score in the range of 400 to 1600 points.

To calculate your Reading & Writing score, count the total number of questions you answered correctly on Module 1 and on Module 2 and add the two numbers together. Exclude the questions that are indicated to be experimental questions as these do not count towards your score. Turn to the Scoring Chart and find the total number of questions you answered correctly.

Using the column for Lower or Upper level module, depending on the level of your 2nd module, identify your SAT® Reading & Writing score.

To calculate your Math score, count the total number of questions you answered correctly on Module 1 and on Module 2 and add the two numbers together. Exclude the questions that are indicated to be experimental questions as these do not count towards your score. Turn to the Scoring Chart and find the total number of questions you answered correctly. Using the column for Lower or Upper level module, depending on the level of your 2nd module, identify your SAT® Math score.

Add together your Reading & Writing score and your Math score to get your Total SAT® Score, in the range of 400 to 1600 points.

# Circle answers below: Reading and Writing Practice Test 1

| Module 1 | Module 2 |
|---|---|

Module 1
1. A B C D
2. A B C D
3. A B C D
4. A B C D
5. A B C D
6. A B C D
7. A B C D
8. A B C D
9. A B C D
10. A B C D
11. A B C D
12 A B C D
13. A B C D
14. A B C D
15. A B C D
16. A B C D
17. A B C D
18. A B C D
19. A B C D
20. A B C D
21. A B C D
22. A B C D
23. A B C D
24. A B C D
25. A B C D
26. A B C D
27. A B C D

Module 2
1. A B C D
2. A B C D
3. A B C D
4. A B C D
5. A B C D
6. A B C D
7. A B C D
8. A B C D
9. A B C D
10. A B C D
11. A B C D
12. A B C D
13. A B C D
14. A B C D
15. A B C D
16. A B C D
17. A B C D
18. A B C D
19. A B C D
20. A B C D
21. A B C D
22. A B C D
23. A B C D
24. A B C D
25. A B C D
26. A B C D
27. A B C D

Write the total number of questions answered correctly in
Module 1: _____ + Module 2: _____ = Total _____

# Circle answers below: Reading and Writing Practice Test 2

| Module 1 | Module 2 |
|---|---|
| 1. A B C D | 1. A B C D |
| 2. A B C D | 2. A B C D |
| 3. A B C D | 3. A B C D |
| 4. A B C D | 4. A B C D |
| 5. A B C D | 5. A B C D |
| 6. A B C D | 6. A B C D |
| 7. A B C D | 7. A B C D |
| 8. A B C D | 8. A B C D |
| 9. A B C D | 9. A B C D |
| 10. A B C D | 10. A B C D |
| 11. A B C D | 11. A B C D |
| 12 A B C D | 12. A B C D |
| 13. A B C D | 13. A B C D |
| 14. A B C D | 14. A B C D |
| 15. A B C D | 15. A B C D |
| 16. A B C D | 16. A B C D |
| 17. A B C D | 17. A B C D |
| 18. A B C D | 18. A B C D |
| 19. A B C D | 19. A B C D |
| 20. A B C D | 20. A B C D |
| 21. A B C D | 21. A B C D |
| 22. A B C D | 22. A B C D |
| 23. A B C D | 23. A B C D |
| 24. A B C D | 24. A B C D |
| 25. A B C D | 25. A B C D |
| 26. A B C D | 26. A B C D |
| 27. A B C D | 27. A B C D |

Write the total number of questions answered correctly in
Module 1: _____ + Module 2: _____ = Total _____

# Reading and Writing Score Chart
*Deduct four points from your total, as there are four experimental questions that do not count towards your score.

| | Lower | Upper | | Lower | Upper |
|---|---|---|---|---|---|
| 1. | 200 | 260 | 26. | 510 | 570 |
| 2. | 200 | 260 | 27. | 520 | 580 |
| 3. | 200 | 260 | 28. | 530 | 590 |
| 4. | 200 | 260 | 29. | 540 | 600 |
| 5. | 200 | 260 | 30. | 550 | 610 |
| 6. | 200 | 280 | 31. | 560 | 620 |
| 7. | 200 | 300 | 32. | 560 | 620 |
| 8. | 200 | 310 | 33. | 570 | 630 |
| 9. | 210 | 330 | 34. | 580 | 640 |
| 10. | 230 | 350 | 35. | 590 | 650 |
| 11. | 240 | 360 | 36. | 610 | 650 |
| 12. | 300 | 420 | 37. | 620 | 660 |
| 13. | 340 | 440 | 38. | 630 | 670 |
| 14. | 360 | 440 | 39. | 640 | 680 |
| 15. | 380 | 460 | 40. | 650 | 690 |
| 16. | 400 | 460 | 41. | 660 | 700 |
| 17. | 420 | 480 | 42. | 670 | 710 |
| 18. | 430 | 490 | 43. | 680 | 720 |
| 19. | 440 | 500 | 44. | 690 | 730 |
| 20. | 450 | 510 | 45. | 700 | 740 |
| 21. | 460 | 520 | 46. | 720 | 760 |
| 22. | 470 | 530 | 47. | 730 | 770 |
| 23. | 480 | 540 | 48. | 740 | 780 |
| 24. | 490 | 550 | 49. | 760 | 800 |
| 25. | 500 | 560 | 50. | 780 | 800 |

# Circle answers below: Math Practice Test 1
For grid-in questions, write answers next to option D

## Module 1

1. A B C D
2. A B C D
3. A B C D
4. A B C D
5. A B C D
6. A B C D
7. A B C D
8. A B C D
9. A B C D
10. A B C D
11. A B C D
12. A B C D
13. A B C D
14. A B C D
15. A B C D
16. A B C D
17. A B C D
18. A B C D
19. A B C D
20. A B C D
21. A B C D
22. A B C D

## Module 2

1. A B C D
2. A B C D
3. A B C D
4. A B C D
5. A B C D
6. A B C D
7. A B C D
8. A B C D
9. A B C D
10. A B C D
11. A B C D
12. A B C D
13. A B C D
14. A B C D
15. A B C D
16. A B C D
17. A B C D
18. A B C D
19. A B C D
20. A B C D
21. A B C D
22. A B C D

Write the total number of questions answered correctly in

Module 1: _____ + Module 2: _____ = Total _____

# Circle answers below: Math Practice Test 2

For grid-in questions, write answers next to option D

| Module 1 | Module 2 |
|---|---|
| 1. A  B  C  D | 1. A  B  C  D |
| 2. A  B  C  D | 2. A  B  C  D |
| 3. A  B  C  D | 3. A  B  C  D |
| 4. A  B  C  D | 4. A  B  C  D |
| 5. A  B  C  D | 5. A  B  C  D |
| 6. A  B  C  D | 6. A  B  C  D |
| 7. A  B  C  D | 7. A  B  C  D |
| 8. A  B  C  D | 8. A  B  C  D |
| 9. A  B  C  D | 9. A  B  C  D |
| 10. A  B  C  D | 10. A  B  C  D |
| 11. A  B  C  D | 11. A  B  C  D |
| 12. A  B  C  D | 12. A  B  C  D |
| 13. A  B  C  D | 13. A  B  C  D |
| 14. A  B  C  D | 14. A  B  C  D |
| 15. A  B  C  D | 15. A  B  C  D |
| 16. A  B  C  D | 16. A  B  C  D |
| 17. A  B  C  D | 17. A  B  C  D |
| 18. A  B  C  D | 18. A  B  C  D |
| 19. A  B  C  D | 19. A  B  C  D |
| 20. A  B  C  D | 20. A  B  C  D |
| 21. A  B  C  D | 21. A  B  C  D |
| 22. A  B  C  D | 22. A  B  C  D |

Write the total number of questions answered correctly in

Module 1: _____  +  Module 2: _____  =  Total _____

# Math Score Chart

**\*Deduct four points from your total, as there are four experimental questions that do not count towards your score.**

| | Lower | Upper | | Lower | Upper |
|---|---|---|---|---|---|
| 1. | 200 | 260 | 21. | 530 | 590 |
| 2. | 200 | 260 | 22. | 540 | 600 |
| 3. | 200 | 260 | 23. | 550 | 610 |
| 4. | 200 | 260 | 24. | 560 | 620 |
| 5. | 200 | 260 | 25. | 570 | 630 |
| 6. | 200 | 260 | 26. | 580 | 640 |
| 7. | 260 | 360 | 27. | 600 | 660 |
| 8. | 300 | 380 | 28. | 610 | 670 |
| 9. | 320 | 400 | 29. | 630 | 690 |
| 10. | 330 | 410 | 30. | 640 | 700 |
| 11. | 360 | 440 | 31. | 660 | 720 |
| 12. | 380 | 440 | 32. | 680 | 740 |
| 13. | 400 | 460 | 33. | 700 | 760 |
| 14. | 420 | 480 | 34. | 720 | 780 |
| 15. | 440 | 500 | 35. | 740 | 800 |
| 16. | 460 | 520 | 36. | 760 | 800 |
| 17. | 470 | 530 | 37. | 770 | 800 |
| 18. | 490 | 550 | 38. | 780 | 800 |
| 19. | 500 | 560 | 39. | 780 | 800 |
| 20. | 510 | 570 | 40. | 780 | 800 |

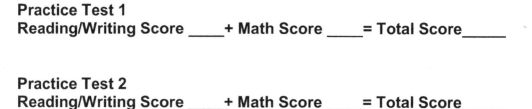

**Practice Test 1**
**Reading/Writing Score _____ + Math Score _____ = Total Score_____**

**Practice Test 2**
**Reading/Writing Score _____ + Math Score _____ = Total Score_____**

# ACCEPTED: COLLEGE PLANNING STRATEGIES FOR HIGH SCHOOL FAMILIES

**by Susan Alaimo**

# DEDICATION

*College is typically one of the most expensive undertakings in a person's life. Collegebound Review is dedicated to providing college-bound students and their parents with the latest information and resources to help them make sound academic and financial choices. Collegebound Review's website includes free PSAT® and SAT® Strategy Guides, a video series on the Strategies of the College Application Process, and weekly blogs on the latest college preparation news for high school parents and students.*

*For 25+ years, Collegebound Review's Ivy League educated instructors have successfully prepared thousands of students for their PSAT®, SAT®, and ACT® exams. Susan Alaimo personally works with a limited number of students each year, advising them through the entire college application process.*

Visit: **CollegeboundReview.com** or Call 908-369-5362

# Accepted: College Planning Strategies
## for High School Families

There's so much information that *all* college-bound students need to think about, starting in their freshman year of high school. They need to begin identifying their areas of passion and pursuing clubs, activities, internships, and experiences that will demonstrate a level of knowledge and commitment once their senior year rolls around. They need to establish a pattern of involvement in volunteer work that, ideally, is compatible with their areas of passion. They need to choose courses as "electives" that may help them identify, or rule out, potential college majors. What students do during their first three years of high school will greatly impact the strength of the college applications they will file early in their senior year.

Many of the college preparation experiences of New Jersey high school students are exactly the same as those of students throughout the country – such as striving for the best grades and preparing for, and taking, SAT® or ACT® exams. But there is much information, specific to New Jersey students, that is particularly invaluable to them. New Jersey college-bound students would do well to learn from the experiences of their peers who preceded them. There are more than 4,000 colleges and universities in the U.S., and no one is able to research and/or visit them all. So, it's extremely beneficial to find out which colleges were most popular with New Jersey students over the course of recent years. (Hint: New Jersey students who leave the state for college head, in large numbers, to the University of Delaware, Penn State, Drexel, and NYU.)

In addition, many states have scholarship programs that are available solely to their residents. Only New Jersey students, for example, are eligible for the NJ Stars (Student Tuition Assistance Reward Scholarship) program that covers the cost of tuition at their home county community college and then provides funds, for those who graduate with a GPA of 3.25 or higher, to move on to any of 26 colleges and universities in New Jersey.

Only New Jersey students are eligible for a vast array of academic, merit, and need-based scholarships: New Jersey Vietnam Veterans' Memorial Foundation Scholarship, Kostic Memorial Foundation Juvenile Diabetes Scholarship, Governor's Urban Scholarship Program, NJCPA (New Jersey Society of Certified Public Accountants) College Scholarship, and the New Jersey State Golf Association Caddie Scholarships.

This guide provides New Jersey students with the strategies, opportunities, and information they need to consider as they navigate through the fascinating, yet sometimes overwhelming, path towards a successful college search.

# Table of Contents

## IV. FILING SUCCESSFUL COLLEGE APPLICATIONS     111

## V. FINANCES, SCHOLARSHIPS, AVOIDING COLLEGE DEBT     157

# Part I. The Early Years of High School

# High School Timeline Eases Student/Parent Stress

Students (and their parents) often wonder what they should be doing during each year of high school to avoid the stress of an anxiety-filled senior year. The truth is that much can be done, starting in the early part of freshman year, to set students on the path of success. Colleges admire students who show longevity in their activities, so the sooner students identify their clubs, sports, volunteer work, or other activities of passion, the longer they have to build a track record of accomplishments.

Freshman year is the perfect time to take on a new musical instrument or sport that might make a student particularly attractive to colleges. Or, students can get involved in an academic-oriented activity, such as Robotics, Model UN, or Science Olympiad. Or, they might join student government, the yearbook committee, the debate team, or the marching band. Another option is to make a commitment to volunteer work which could earn a 50% to 100% tuition scholarship to The College of New Jersey which seeks "Bonner Community Scholars" who complete 300 volunteer hours each college year.

By sophomore year, students should map out a tentative four-year academic schedule. If they hope to get through Calculus in high school, are they on track to do so? If not, they may want to double up on their math courses one year or take a course during summer study. If planning to apply to colleges as a STEM major, they should aim to complete a full array of science courses, ideally including some at the Advanced Placement level. Sophomores should also prepare for the October PSAT®, as it will provide a helpful analysis as to their strengths and weaknesses before they go on to take the Junior year PSAT® which also serves as the National Merit Scholarship Qualifying Test (NMSQT). Hopefully, Sophomores are actively pursuing the activities of choice that they identified the previous year, gaining increased expertise.

High school Juniors start feeling the crunch of preparing for their transition to college. If they haven't already done so, Juniors should start preparing for, and taking, the SAT® exam as they can take it as many times as they like and submit their highest scores to colleges. The SAT® is given each year in October, November, December, March, May, June, and August. It's ideal for students to have completed the SAT® process by the time they begin Senior year. Juniors should also pay close attention to their grades, as it is often the last report card that colleges see prior to admitting (or rejecting) applicants. Students may also want to prepare a resume, as it will help them recall all their high school activities when it's time to list them on college applications. Many colleges even have space on their application for a resume to be uploaded.

During the first two months of Senior year students should carefully prepare, and submit, their college applications. This will allow them to meet Early Action and/or Early Decision deadlines, which are typically November 1st, and will frequently increase their chances of acceptance. Students should be sure to keep up their grades during their senior year, even after they have been accepted to their college of choice, as a serious decline in grades may result in a withdrawal of college acceptance.

By keeping track of all their academic responsibilities and applying to colleges during the first couple of months, students can truly enjoy their senior year – often the last one they will live at home with their families.

# The Importance of Volunteer Work

One quality that college admissions officers particularly value in applicants is a demonstrated commitment to volunteer work. High school students should become involved, early on, in community service work and should ideally choose an area that coincides with their interests and potential college major. Students seeking a career in medicine should consider volunteering at a hospital or, even more impressive, becoming an EMT. Students passionate about history could volunteer at a museum or even join the cast of volunteers that recreate Revolutionary War battles and Washington Crossing the Delaware.

Athletes may want to coach younger players in basketball, football, or soccer through their town's recreation program. Other options are to volunteer at a local YMCA, or get involved with Special Olympics, headquartered in Lawrenceville, NJ. Scouts can choose to mentor a younger troop in their community. Dancers can offer free lessons in their area of specialty – Irish Step Dancing, Indian Dance, Jazz – to students at afterschool centers.

Students who have not yet become engaged in "giving back" can likely find an activity of interest on the Jersey Cares website jerseycares.org which includes a volunteer opportunity calendar featuring a multitude of do-good options.

DoSomething.org, one of the largest organizations helping teens get involved in worthy causes, released a study tying volunteerism to college admissions. The results indicated that admissions officers place a high value on a student's long-term commitment to a cause or organization. Consistency is the key, as colleges prefer students who support one cause over a lengthy period of time during which they demonstrate dedication and perseverance.

Another source of volunteer opportunities is Zooniverse.org. This site offers countless options for students to work remotely, which became even more appealing during the Covid pandemic. Among its many unique projects is one that involves measuring evolution by becoming a "Squirrel Mapper," pinpointing gray squirrels and black squirrels in a geographic region. Another project, "Penguin Watch," involves watching timelapse images of Rockhopper penguin colonies in Argentina to study their breeding behaviors in the context of climate change.

Students looking to spread their wings often find that volunteer work provides a great opportunity to travel cheaply while doing some good. Ideally, students should choose to visit a part of the world that fascinates them and a type of volunteer work that coincides with their interests and potential life work.

The travel-abroad site *GoOverseas.com* offers students the chance to read about thousands of programs, ask questions of travelers who have been there, and apply to programs of interest. There are more than 15,000 programs to choose from, including *Panda Volunteer Experience* in China, *Teach Music* in South Africa, or *Climate Change at the Arctic's Edge* and *Wildlife Rehab: Rescue Orphaned and Injured Animals* in Canada. Other programs are offered in Australia, Thailand, Nepal, Costa Rica, Peru, India, Ghana, Ecuador, Kenya, Tanzania, Guatemala, and a multitude of other locations.

The opportunities are almost limitless. Volunteer programs are offered in a wide variety of fields, including elephant, primate or sea turtle conservation; orphan, elderly, or disabled care; computer literacy; refugee or disaster relief; women's rights; reforestation; veterinary service; education; agriculture; business; teaching; tourism; and many more. In reality, it would be difficult for a student *not* to find an area of interest.

Although there are volunteer opportunities abroad at any time of year, there are many that exclusively run during the summer. For example, students can live in beautiful Tenerife, Spain and work with the island's threatened whale and dolphin populations. Or, students can choose to live with host families in Zambia and teach local students, work with orphans, help out at hospitals, or participate in construction projects. Volunteers seeking a chance to see the wildlife, beaches, historical sites and mountains in the Andes, Peru, can work in the heart of the Amazon on a rainforest conservation program.

Colleges favor students with a history of volunteerism with the hope that their commitment will enrich the college community, where there are limitless opportunities for involvement. The Office of Student Involvement and Leadership at Rutgers University hosts more than 550 student organizations. It also offers students limitless opportunities to serve others, both nationally and internationally, through "Rutgers Alternative Breaks" service trips.

The College of New Jersey (TCNJ) offers between 50 to 100 percent tuition scholarships to students who make a substantial commitment to volunteerism by becoming Bonner Community Scholars. These students choose to focus on one area of service, such as hunger, homelessness, the environment, juvenile justice, immigrant services, or urban education, and provide 300 hours of meaningful service over the course of a year, combining volunteerism with their academic experiences.

Aside from its boost to their college applications, volunteerism is extremely beneficial to students in many ways. It tends to make them aware, and grateful, for the many blessings of their lives. It empowers young people to realize that they can make a difference in the world. It helps them put their priorities in order and use their time productively. It helps students develop vital skills, such as working collaboratively with others towards a mutual goal. It often has the surprising effect of helping students identify their life calling, and with it their college major! Admissions officers used to consider it a bonus to find community service work listed on a college application. Now it's an expectation, with extra points for demonstrated levels of commitment and initiative.

# Showcasing a Unique Talent

Years ago, college-bound students were advised to present themselves as well-rounded individuals on their college applications. So, while in high school they would join a multitude of activities, ranging from sports to music to academic oriented clubs. Those days are long gone. Colleges are no longer looking for renaissance students who have spread themselves thin, engaged in a multitude of activities. Rather, colleges are seeking students with a particular talent or expertise that they developed over a lengthy period of time.

High school students should try to identify their passion, and then devote time and effort to becoming the very best they can be. If athletics is their choice, it's a good idea to keep in mind some of the less popular sports where competition is less intense. Unless they have a natural talent and truly excel at soccer, basketball, or football, it is unlikely that these extremely popular sports will give them an edge in the college admission process. According to ScholarshipStats.com, the percent of high school athletes who go on to compete in college have the best odds for men's lacrosse (15.1%), baseball (12.4%), and ice hockey (10%). For women, the best numbers appeared for ice hockey (22%) and lacrosse (14.2%). Overall, statistics indicate that only 7% of high school athletes go on to play a sport in college and less than 2% of high school athletes go on to play at NCAA Division I schools.

A similar strategy can be applied to music, as orchestras and marching bands attract large numbers of students at most high schools. Here, too, a little advanced planning can make a big difference. A high school conductor once referred to the middle section of his orchestra as "Scholarship Row." This is the area that seated students playing oboes, bassoons, bass clarinets, baritone saxophones, and tubas.

Students with a bent for dancing might want to develop their skills in a specialized area such as Bollywood, Hip Hop, Jazz, or Irish

Step Dancing.  While having fun advancing their talent, they may end up on the Bollywood team at Rutgers, Rowan or Penn State, the Hip Hop Team at Ohio State or University of Delaware, the Jazz Team at University of Michigan, or the Irish Dance Team at Villanova, Fordham, Georgetown, or Boston College.

Students who spent years in scouting can use this worthwhile activity as a launching pad for college.  While it's very impressive to earn the highest level Eagle Scout or Gold Award, there are tens of thousands of students who reach the top tier each year.  To make their achievement truly noteworthy to colleges, students should carefully select their culminating project to ensure that it will have a long-term, positive impact on its intended community.

Some students pursue more individualized activities.  A Florida student gained attention for being offered more than a million dollars in scholarship money.  The quality that differentiated her from most of her peers was that she had been an equestrian rider since the first grade.  After breaking her femur in freshman year, she had picked up "dressage."  This is when a rider and horse perform a series of precise, memorized movements.  She had earned second place in a national competition.

Close to a thousand students each year are not only accepted to, but also awarded free tuition and housing at, 19 prestigious universities due to their work as golf caddies.  Other students, talented in cartooning or video game innovation, are accepted to colleges and awarded scholarship money each year by the National Cartoonist Society Foundation and the Academy of Interactive Arts & Sciences Association.

By choosing an activity that is both fun and purposeful, students can enjoy their afterschool hours while putting themselves on the right track to ultimately impressing college admissions officers. The key is for students to stand out from the pack, in whatever activity they choose, and make sure college admissions officers are aware of their talent.

# Choosing an Impressive Course Schedule

Throughout their high school years, students are making decisions that will ultimately impact the success of their college applications. Most notably, they are choosing the high school courses they will take, and the level of difficulty of these courses.

There are certainly guidelines required by the State of New Jersey, including four years of English and Physical Education/Health, three years of Math, Science and Social Studies, and an array of courses in World Languages, Visual or Performing Arts, and Financial Literacy. But students are given great latitude as to the specific courses taken within these fields and the level of rigorousness of these courses. Also, students with the goal of enrolling in an elite college or university should seek to surpass the minimum high school graduation requirements.

Regarding Math, for example, students are required to take Algebra I, Geometry, and one higher level course. But many colleges strongly favor students who have studied both Pre-Calculus and Calculus during their high school years, particularly if they will be pursuing a major in Business, Engineering, Architecture, or other math-intensive field. Such students need to carefully plan their four-year course of study, as they may need to double-up on Math during one high school year or take a summer course for which they will be given credit.

Electives are another area in which high school students have a great deal of latitude and an opportunity to impress college admissions officers. Students considering a major in Business or Economics should study both Macroeconomics and Micro-economics during their high school years. It's one of the most popular majors at many elite colleges and universities and can serve as a "back door" into universities with extremely competitive business schools, as economics is generally a part of the College of Arts and Sciences.

Students anticipating a career in Psychology should take a course in that field. Those planning a future as Physical Therapists, Physician's Assistants, or Physical Education/Health Teachers should choose to study Anatomy & Physiology. There is often a supplementary essay on college applications asking students to explain why they have chosen their particular major. By taking a high school course in the field, they will be able to rationalize their choice.

Students should pursue the most rigorous course of study for their abilities, focusing on their areas of interest. Most local high schools offer an array of Advanced Placement (AP) courses, for which students may be awarded college credits based on their performance on end-of-year AP exams. Students considering a pre-med track in college would do well to undertake AP Biology and/or AP Chemistry. Students anticipating a future career in law may favor AP Government & Politics and/or AP US History.

The courses chosen by high school students, and their level of rigor, will certainly be noticed by college admissions officers.

# Stretching Academically

Colleges are most attracted to students who demonstrate intellectual curiosity. Seeking out, and becoming engaged in, academically enriching activities outside of the classroom serves many benefits for high school students. First of all, it helps them stand out from their peers, most of whom are taking the standard course load dictated by the State of New Jersey. Secondly, it helps students identify potential college majors by becoming familiar with material in the field. For example, many high school students consider psychology for their college studies because they like helping to solve their friends' problems. A college-level course in psychology, the study of the brain, is often eye opening.

Likewise, many high school students think about becoming physical therapists. Who wouldn't want a career healing athletes on the Giants, Jets, Eagles, Nets or Yankees rosters? Often, a course in human anatomy and physiology puts this potential major into perspective. Expanding the mind by seeking knowledge in any area of interest helps students become more proficient and adept learners.

Students seeking academic enrichment have a vast array of options. Many high school students take courses at local community colleges where they are most welcome, and often offered a discounted tuition. Other students take courses online, where the opportunities are almost limitless. High school students in New Jersey can actually sit at home on their computers and take courses such as *Medical Neuroscience* from Duke University, *Introduction to Computer Science & Programming* from M.I.T., *Understanding Research Methods* from The University of London, *or Particle Physics* from The University of Geneva.

These are just a sample of the thousands of college courses that are offered through online services from many of the most prestigious colleges and universities in the U.S. and 28 other countries. Students can typically explore lectures and non-graded material at no cost. However, there is often a charge if students submit assignments to be graded, or if students want to receive a certificate upon completion of a course.

A great source on virtual courses is *edX.org,* which was founded by Harvard University and M.I.T. as an online learning destination to offer high-quality courses from the world's top universities. Today, it offers more than 4,000 courses from over 250 leading institutions worldwide.

A similar online learning destination is *coursera.org* which offers more than 5,800 courses. Among the most popular topics are Computer Science, Business, Data Science, Physical Science & Engineering, Social Science, and Arts & Humanities.

Both of these online sites host courses in several languages, including English, Spanish, French and Chinese, and offer introductory, intermediate, and advanced level courses.

These courses can be extremely beneficial to high school students trying to identify a potential college major. By taking an online course in a field of possible interest, students can assess if they enjoy the course of study and seem to have a natural talent to succeed. Immersing themselves in these courses, whether taking *Game Theory* from Stanford University or *Algorithms* from Princeton University, is a sure way for college-bound students to add an impressive element to their college applications.

Colleges and universities greatly value the quality of intellectual curiosity and will take special note of students who took courses, outside of the required high school curriculum, on their own personal time. What college admissions officer wouldn't be impressed with an essay written by a student who studied *Entrepreneurship in Emerging Economies* or *Introduction to Artificial Intelligence with Python* with a Harvard University professor?

# Benefits of Virtual College Touring

Moving onto college is a huge step for any student. For most, it is the first time they are actually choosing their own school, the city where they will live, the academic, social and cultural climate they will be surrounded by, and the future life work for which they will prepare. Students, and their parents, should recognize the enormity of this next chapter in their lives and gather as much information as possible.

It's never too early for students to start considering all the options that lie ahead. In fact, if they'd like to tour multiple Ivy League schools in one afternoon, while lounging in their bedroom sipping hot chocolate, that's certainly an option. Sites such as appily.com provide 360-degree virtual tours of colleges worldwide, sharing the academic, cultural, and social experiences offered on more than one thousand campuses.

If you choose to start at Harvard University, for example, you can enjoy a virtual tour around the scenic campus, experiencing the research centers, classrooms, library, and Harvard Square.

Duke University is another elite school featured on appily.com. A tour of this campus, ranked one of the most beautiful in the country, includes the iconic Duke Chapel and its 210 foot tower that soars above the West Campus. Also featured is the famed Cameron Stadium.

Another popular site, campustours.com, offers video tours, interactive campus maps, and mobile walking tours of colleges and universities nationwide, including 33 two and four year schools in New Jersey. More than 30 million students to date have engaged with this site.

While nothing can replace the actual experience of walking the grounds of a college and interacting with its students, faculty and staff, virtual tours are a great tool for previewing college campuses and seeing all the resources and amenities that they offer. Students should then take the next step, for any college they find appealing, and visit the college's website. Here they can gather much crucial information: list of majors offered, admission requirements, average SAT®/ACT® scores and GPA of accepted students, and cost of attendance.

Students should make a list of questions regarding each college that piques their interest, and then reach out to an admissions officer at the school. This is the basis of establishing a relationship with the college and showing demonstrated interest. Students should be sure that the questions they ask are specific, and that the answers cannot easily be found on the college's website.

It's important to keep a record of virtual tours and any interaction with each college, as this information will come in handy when the time comes to fill out applications. Colleges often ask why you are applying to their school, and whether or not you have visited. The more information a student can provide demonstrating a knowledge of the school and enthusiasm for joining the college community, the greater the likelihood of gaining acceptance.

Thanks to technology, students can still tour far away colleges even when a road trip is not in the picture.

# Use Vacation Time Wisely

The summer provides a unique opportunity for students to engage in meaningful activities that will demonstrate their commitment to a particular field of study and help them stand out from their peers. This can be accomplished through participation in extracurricular activities, volunteer opportunities, or enrollment in specialized courses.

Students seeking acceptance into a particular course of study – business, engineering, pre-med, physical therapy – are often asked to write a supplemental essay about their "experiences" that have led to their passion for the field. Summer is the ideal time to shadow a mentor in the field, participate in an internship, or engage in some pre-professional program.

Experience can also be gained through immersion in volunteer work. Students seeking remote engagement should visit Zooniverse.org, which provides online opportunities to work in collaboration with professional researchers in a multitude of fields in science and the humanities. Additionally, hundreds of in-person volunteer opportunities are posted on jerseycares.org, which hosts a daily calendar of projects in a wide variety of fields.

Another popular use of the summer break is to take a college course or two. Many elite colleges and universities "invite" thousands of high school students – and sometimes even middle schoolers – to spend a portion of their summer living on campus, attending classes, and experiencing the life of an undergraduate.

Princeton, Harvard, Yale, Columbia, Cornell, The University of Pennsylvania, Brown, Georgetown, Johns Hopkins, Stanford, UCLA, NYU, Duke, Boston College, and scores of other colleges and universities open their campus each summer to teens who later dream of returning for their college experience.

The problem is that the admission process for most summer programs can barely be considered competitive, while the admission process for undergraduate acceptance is truly daunting at many of these same institutions. Often students and their parents are under the false impression that attending a summer program for high school students at an elite college will ultimately help them gain acceptance for their undergraduate studies. A *Washington Monthly* article, titled "The Pre-College Racket," reported that, according to professional admissions consultants, attending a pre-college program seldom offers a special benefit or is particularly prestigious on college applications. These summer programs are often quite costly, with the price dependent on its length and number of courses. But parents can expect to spend several thousand dollars for a multi-week stay.

Of course, there are good reasons for students to attend pre-college summer programs. If there is a college to which a student is considering applying "early decision," spending a few weeks on the campus during the prior summer can often affirm or refute that it's the student's ideal school.

Summer programs are also extremely beneficial in familiarizing students with academic fields that they are considering for their college major. For example, students interested in psychology had options, during the Summer of '23, to attend the "Psychology Institute" at Wake Forest University, engage in the "Clinical Neuroscience Immersion Experience" at Stanford University, or study, "Introduction to Psychology: The Frontiers of Psychological Inquiry" at Cornell University. Other psychology courses were offered, through pre-college programs, at Brown University, Duke University, Georgetown University, Johns Hopkins University, and a multitude of other schools.

Similarly, many high school students seeking to familiarize themselves with different fields of engineering attended pre-college programs at Boston University, University of Illinois

Urbana Champaign, University of Maryland, Rutgers, NJIT, and four campuses of the University of California.

A summer Engineering Exploration Camp was hosted by the Society of Women Engineers at the University of Michigan, and at Cornell University the CURIE Academy educated female students on career opportunities in engineering.

Minority Introduction to Engineering and Science (MITES) programs were offered at M.I.T. and Purdue, while a no-cost Summer Academy for Math and Science (SAMS) was available at Carnegie Mellon University for students from under-represented communities to explore and improve their STEM knowledge.

As long as students and parents have realistic expectations of the benefits of pre-college summer programs, they can certainly offer an exciting experience for students looking forward to their college years.

Students considering a specific college major can also demonstrate their interest in the field by taking an online course at a renowned university almost anywhere in the world. For example, edX.org offers more than 4,000 options including *Bioethics: The Law, Medicine, and Ethics of Reproductive Technologies and Genetics* from Harvard University, *Constitutional Interpretation* at Princeton University, *Quantum Mechanics for Scientists and Engineers 1* from Stanford University, and *Becoming an Entrepreneur* or *Supply Chain Analytics* at MIT.

Similarly, more than 7,000 online courses are offered at Coursera.org. Both sites offer many course options free of charge.

Summer is also a perfect time for students to explore their creative talents. Students planning to major in the visual arts may want to spend the summer developing their portfolio. There are National Portfolio Days throughout the country each fall, including ones in

Philadelphia and Manhattan, where college representatives critique the work of high school students. Students who prepare in advance can maximize this opportunity to present their work to an array of colleges and then use the feedback to improve their work and better their chances of ultimately gaining acceptance to their dream school.

Students can also use their summer leisure time to create a "passion project" – an endeavor that is uniquely their own. They can build a portfolio highlighting their accomplishments, create a film, or write and self-publish a book at little-to-no cost, with the help of Amazon's self-publishing site. They can identify, and fill, a need in the community or organize a local fundraiser. They can create a website as a resource for students, or launch a free tutoring program, via Zoom or in person at the local library. The options are limited only by one's ingenuity.

# Part II. It's All About "The Test"

# Why and When Students Should Take the PSAT®

Hundreds of thousands of high school students throughout the country take the PSAT® exam each October, but many don't understand its significance. Students and parents often believe the "P" in PSAT® stands for practice and that the test is merely a trial run for the all-important SAT® exam. In reality, the "P" does not stand for "practice," "preliminary," or anything else, and it's so much more than a student's first attempt at a college entrance exam.

Another name for the PSAT® is the NMSQT® which *does* stand for something -- National Merit Scholarship Qualifying Test. High school *juniors* who take the PSAT®/NMSQT® are on the official route of entry to the National Merit Scholarship Program. Fifty thousand high scoring students each year ultimately qualify for program recognition – which carries considerable prestige. Of these students, two-thirds end up receiving Letters of Commendation, but are not awarded scholarship money. One-third of these students ultimately qualify as semi-finalists and move on to compete for National Merit Scholarships which are awarded to 7,500 students annually.

The majority of high school juniors take the PSAT®/NMSQT®, not only to be eligible for recognition and scholarship money, but also to get on the radar of colleges nationwide. The College Board, which produces the PSAT® (and SAT® exams) shares information provided by students, such as their current GPA and potential college major, with colleges and universities. These schools often send informational material, and sometimes college application fee waivers, to students whom they identify to be potential applicants. It's encouraging for students to receive unsolicited information from colleges that seem eager to attract them.

High school sophomores, and even freshmen, often choose to take the PSAT®. The exam is strictly a trial run for them as their scores are not eligible for National Merit consideration until they are juniors.  Since the same academic material is covered on the PSAT® and SAT® exams, students find it ideal to prepare prior to taking their PSAT® as it then benefits them for both exams.

# Facts of the SAT®

Some two million students take the SAT® each year at nearly 7,000 test centers in more than 170 countries. For many test-takers, their scores will play a major role in determining their college options and the amount of money they will be awarded by the college of their choice for each of their college years. The SAT® scores of applicants are one of the most important criteria in their acceptance decisions, according to many college admissions officers.

Colleges recognize that the students seeking admission to their school have had vastly different high school experiences. Some attended local public schools, some attended prestigious private schools, some were home-schooled and graded by their parents. Even within the same school, some teachers are easier graders and allow students to drop their lowest grade, re-take exams, and do extra-credit work in their quest for impressive grades. Other teachers average out test scores to the hundredth of a point and grade students accordingly. Therefore, college admissions officers cannot focus strictly on the GPA's (grade point averages) of their applicants.

Colleges know that the SAT® is the one level playing field on which they can compare all applicants who hail from a wide range of educational environments. So, the scores carry significant weight in the admissions process. Students take the same test, and it is marked on a curve placing students in competition with their peers.
An alternative test, which will be discussed later, is the ACT®.

It's not a secret as to what's on the SAT®. In fact, College Board publishes a book, *The Official Digital SAT Study Guide*. It includes four practice exams mirroring exactly what students will face on their test. Students who want to practice taking the digital test, to mimic the real experience, can download the Bluebook digital testing application on a Windows laptop or tablet, an Apple laptop, or an iPad, on College Board's website. Additional online practice is available through Khan Academy.

The most basic strategy for acing the SAT® is to become thoroughly familiar with the test material ahead of time. By taking practice exams, students will be well on their way to earning an impressive score on the day of their real test.

The SAT® is comprised of two Reading and Writing modules followed by two Math modules.

The Reading and Writing modules are each comprised of 27 questions to be answered within a time frame of 32 minutes. The questions on the first module vary greatly as to the level of difficulty. Depending on how well a student performs on the first module, he/she will be given a second module of either easier or harder questions. Of course, this will impact the final score.

The Reading and Writing modules are made up of one paragraph stories, each followed by one multiple choice question. Students should read the question prior to reading the paragraph so they know what to look for. Some questions ask students to choose a word that best fills in the blank. Other questions ask which fact is true about a character in the story, or what is the main idea of the text. Additional questions focus on proper grammar and punctuation.

Students should answer each question as they work through the module. There is no deduction for wrong answers, so students should take an educated guess, when necessary. Students should carefully read the question, then the paragraph, and then the four answer options: A through D. If the student has a favorite answer, it should be recorded. If not, the student should eliminate any answer he/she does not like, and then take a guess between those that are left. There are no "trick questions," so students should choose the answer they feel is strongest. It doesn't pay for students to skip questions with the intention of going back to them later, as they will then have to read the entire paragraph again.

There are two "experimental" questions on each module that do not count towards a student's score. But there is no way to know which questions are the experimental ones, so all should be answered.

Reading and Writing modules are followed by two Math modules, each comprised of 22 questions to be answered within a time frame of 35 minutes. Here again, the questions on the first module vary greatly as to the level of difficulty. Depending on how well a student performs on the first module, he/she will be given a second module of either easier or harder questions, which will impact the final score.

The Math modules consist mostly of multiple-choice questions, with options A through D, but about 25% of the questions are open-ended. On these questions, students need to record their answer according to specific rules. Students should look at practice tests, in advance, to become familiar with these rules so as not to lose any time deciphering them on test day.

Students are allowed to use a calculator on both Math modules. They should bring their own, but are also allowed to use the online one built into the test. Students are provided with scrap paper and should use it to draw diagrams, write out solutions step-by-step, and do anything helpful to make the questions more visual.

The Math covered on the SAT is basic problem solving, Algebra I and II, and a few questions in the areas of Geometry and Trigonometry. Typically, the Trig question tests students on the fact that, in a right triangle, sin x = cos y. There are no Pre-Calculus or Calculus questions on the test.

Students should remember that there is a box of formulas provided at the beginning of each Math module that they are allowed to refer to while working on these questions. While it includes all the Geometry formulas they need to know, it excludes two formulas that are frequently tested on the SAT®. One is the center-radius form of the circle equation and the other is the quadratic formula.

As there is no deduction for wrong answers, students should answer every question. To earn the best score possible, students should initially skip any Math questions that they do not know how to do, and then go back to them later after answering the rest of the questions.

There will be a countdown clock on the digital test, letting students know how their time is progressing. When the end is approaching, students should take a guess on any questions they had not yet answered.

Since there are four choices (A through D) for most questions, even random guessing will – according to the Laws of Probability – result in a correct answer 25% of the time.

Students earn a score, in the range of 200 to 800 points, for both Reading/Writing and Math. These scores are added together to get a total SAT® Score in the range of 400 to 1600 points.

The best overall strategy for the entire SAT® is to prepare, well in advance of test day. Utilize exams written by College Board in order to be proficient in the material tested and knowledgeable of the directions and format for each module. Collegebound Review's PSAT® and SAT® Exam Strategy Guide can be downloaded free of charge at CollegeboundReview.com

# How Many Times Should Students Take the SAT®?

By the time students reach high school, they are tired of taking standardized tests. But this is just the time when students need to be most diligent. Standardized tests in students' earlier years are most important for their school and school district, to determine if educational goals are being met and to rank how the school/district compares to others in the state and nation. But when it comes to the SAT® exam, things get personal.

The SAT® is a standardized test that is marked on a curve, placing college-bound students in competition with each other. Students get two scores, each in the range of 200 to 800 points, with a total SAT® score in the range of 400 to 1600 points. While a "combined" score of 1,000 may get students into some schools, the colleges most popular with many New Jersey students are seeking substantially higher SAT® scores. For example, the mid-range SAT® score of accepted students is 1350 at Rutgers (New Brunswick), 1390 at Lehigh, 1420 at University of Maryland and Villanova, and 1510 at NYU.

But it's not just for college acceptance that SAT® scores are so important. It's also the cost of college that is greatly impacted by SAT® scores. A college education is one of the largest expenses that most families will face in their lifetime. The amount of money they will pay is often directly correlated to their child's SAT® scores, as almost all colleges award merit aid (scholarships) based on SAT® scores since it's the only level playing field on which to compare students from thousands of different high schools and from very varied educational experiences.

The good news for students is that they can take the SAT® as many times as they like, and colleges never know. It's given seven times each year: October, November, December, March, May, June, and August. When the time comes to submit college applications and send SAT® scores, students log into their College Board account where all their SAT® scores will be recorded.

Students are allowed to "select scores" by checking off which of their prior test scores they want to send to colleges. Even if a college says it wants to see all scores, students do not have to oblige. Basically, students get unlimited "do-overs" and should make the most of that opportunity.

When students first register (on Collegeboard.org) to take the SAT®, they have the option of listing a few colleges to receive their test scores free of charge. Students should leave this section blank, as they do not know prior to taking the test whether they will get scores that are worthy of being shared. After students have taken the SAT® for the last time, they should log into their College Board account and select only their highest scores to be sent to colleges. The current cost is $14 for each college submission.

While taking the SAT® may not be the most pleasant use of a Saturday morning, the payoff can be significant. Most colleges allocate merit scholarship awards based on SAT® scores. So, by taking the test several times and submitting one's highest scores, students have the best chance of earning impressive scholarship funds for their freshman year of college. These awards are typically renewed for the student's next three years, as long as a minimum GPA is maintained.

Of course, preparation is the key to students improving their scores. It's not a secret as to what material is covered on the SAT®. By learning the strategies for each test section, practicing with official College Board test material, and having wrong answers carefully explained, students can often increase their SAT® scores by hundreds of points – greatly minimizing the college debt they (or their families) need to incur.

Taking the SAT® is currently an investment of $60 and a Saturday morning – but it offers the best potential for maximizing the scholarship money that your college of choice will offer.

# True Story of College Board's SAT® Curve

On the national news one evening, students were televised protesting their SAT® scores. They didn't believe they had been graded fairly on the June 2018 SAT® exam and they called on everyone from Donald Trump to Ellen DeGeneres to intercede on their behalf. In looking back on their scores, in comparison to those of students who performed in a similar manner on other SAT® exams, the power of the SAT® curve is undeniable.

Twins who took different SAT® exams reported that one sibling got five math questions wrong on the March 2018 exam and earned a score of 760. Her sister missed six math questions on the June 2018 exam and earned a score of 670. The question raised was, "How can one wrong answer result in a score 90 points lower?"

Two young men whom I personally prepared for the SAT® each answered 56 of the 58 math questions correctly on their respective exams. The student who accomplished this feat on the June 2018 exam scored 720, while the student who did the same on the August 2018 exam scored 790. When the goal is to gain acceptance to an elite university, a 70 point "discrepancy" can have a profound impact.

The problem is the curve, although College Board doesn't call it a "curve," but rather an "equating system." Students taking the SAT® get one point for each correct answer. (No points are deducted for incorrect answers.) The points are totaled for each test section, giving students a raw score for Math and Reading/Writing. Then, a Conversion Chart is used to change a raw score into an actual test score. But the Conversion Chart is adjusted for each test, based on the number of questions that all test-takers answered correctly. So, if a certain SAT® exam turns out to be unusually easy for students, or the test-takers a certain month are unusually smart, then students need to answer a greater number of questions correctly to score a 700, for example, than they would have on a different SAT® exam.

What can students do to make the best of College Board's equating system? They can take the SAT® several times to have the best chance of getting in on a favorable curve. And they should never have their test scores sent to colleges until they are sure they have taken the SAT® for the very last time. Then, students can pick and choose exactly which scores to send – ignoring any that were negatively impacted by the curve.

# How "Super-Scoring" Works

High school students throughout the world all want to get the highest scores possible when taking the SAT® as it greatly impacts college admissions and scholarship awards. Students get two separate scores on an SAT® exam: Reading/Writing and Math. The scores for each of these two areas range from 200 to 800. Students add their scores together for a "combined" SAT® score in the range of 400 to 1600 points.

Many colleges report that they "super-score" and will consider the highest Reading/Writing score from one SAT® exam and the highest Math score from another. Problems arise when students misinterpret this policy. Students often believe that when it comes time to submit their SAT® scores, they can choose to send their highest module scores from different SAT® dates, and that is all the testing information colleges will receive. With that premise in mind, some students will take an SAT® exam and only focus on the Reading/Writing modules, not putting any effort into the Math modules. On a subsequent SAT® they flip their strategy and focus on Math modules, not worrying about their Reading/Writing score. Their thinking is that they will ultimately "super-score."

These students are in for a rude awakening when they log into their College Board account to send SAT® scores to colleges. While they can certainly submit their test scores from two (or more) SAT® exams, there is no way to submit a score for only one area of a test. So, colleges will see the impressive Reading/Writing score on one exam, and the notable Math score on another exam. But they will also see the very mediocre, or worse, scores on the areas students thought wouldn't matter.

There is no way to know, in advance, which SAT® exam may turn out to be harder or easier or have a tougher or more lenient curve. So, students should take the SAT® exam several times, trying their hardest on each module every time. Then, if "super-scoring" happens to benefit them, it is an extra perk.

# Maximize Scores by Testing Early

The advice of *U.S. News & World Report*, whose guidebook *Best Colleges* is basically the Bible to the college industry, is for students to start taking the SAT® exam early in their high school years for several reasons.

First of all, students can take the SAT® as many times as they want and colleges never know how many times they've taken the test. When the time comes for students to send their scores to colleges, they can choose their highest scores, even "super-scoring" (mixing and matching), to utilize their best Math score from one test and their best Reading/Writing score from another test.

Another advantage to students who start taking the SAT® early is that their first test can serve as a baseline, indicating what areas they need to hone. Then, as students practice for subsequent tests, either on their own or with the help of a private tutor or preparation course, they can get measurable results and track their improvement. It's also a good idea to get that first SAT® experience, which is likely to be stress-ridden, out of the way in order to be a bit more relaxed at future sittings.

Students can use early SAT® scores to influence their choice of high school courses. Those struggling in Math would want to get through Algebra I and II early in their high school years, as a substantial number of SAT® Math questions are directly related to Algebra. If weakness in reading comprehension or grammar are resulting in low scores on the Reading/Writing modules, students can likewise choose classes to strengthen these literary skills.

Even students who may not be bound for a four-year college should prepare for, and take, the SAT® exam. Although community "junior" colleges typically do not require SAT® scores for admission, these test scores are required to be eligible for many college scholarships. Respectable SAT® scores can also exempt college applicants from taking placement exams that may result in a requirement to take "remedial" (non-credit) courses. In addition, if a student seeks to transfer from a community college to a four-year college without first completing a certain number of credits, the college the student is applying to will often want to review SAT® scores. Even after graduating from college, students are often asked by potential employers, such as consulting firms, software companies, and financial institutions, to dig up their SAT® scores.

Taking the SAT® early can give all students, regardless of their academic strengths or weaknesses, the time and motivation needed to improve their scores. Students can continue taking the SAT® as many times as they want throughout their high school years. The test is offered each year in October, November, December, March, May, June, and August. College Board keeps a record of each student's scores. When the time comes to apply to their colleges of choice, students simply log into their College Board account and pick and choose the scores they want to send. By preparing diligently for this all-important test, and taking it as many times as necessary to reach their potential, students can greatly increase their chances of getting accepted into their college of choice – hopefully with scholarship money to help foot the bill.

# Power of Impressive SAT® Scores

Jeff Bezos, the billionaire founder of Amazon, is one of the most famous advocates of using SAT® scores in the hiring process. "Hiring only the best and brightest was key to Amazon's success," claimed Bezos, who scored highly on standardized tests from the time he was a young child.

Amazon is not the only big-name company to request SAT® scores of its job applicants. According to *The Wall Street Journal*, impressive consulting firms such as McKinsey & Company, and leading banks including Goldman Sachs, are among the companies that ask about SAT® scores on their job applications. And this is not the case just for recent college grads seeking their first full-time jobs. Mid-life workers who have garnered real world life and work experience, for whom their high school SAT® experience is a decades old memory, are often asked to report their scores.

The reason SAT® scores may stick with people throughout their lives is that it's both standardized and objective. Everyone takes the SAT® at approximately the same time in life with roughly the same level of education (16 to 18 year olds in junior or senior year of high school). The test is marked on a curve, so an individual's SAT® score represents how well he or she scored in comparison with peers. For this reason, SAT® scores are even a criterion for a number of college internships as well as admission into some graduate school programs.

Jonathan Wai, an intelligence expert and former researcher at Duke University's *Talent Identification Program (TIP)*, said the SAT® is considered to be a measure of "general intelligence and general ability." He added that research has shown that general ability "actually predicts occupational success across a range of occupations."

# What About the ACT®?

High school students planning to attend college know that a standardized college admission exam lies in their future. For almost a century, the test of choice was the SAT®. It was created in 1926 to allow college-bound students to take one entrance exam for several universities, instead of taking a separate entrance exam for each university to which they applied. Its purpose, also, was to provide equal opportunity for all students to demonstrate their skills and knowledge regardless of their economic status and their specific high school curriculum. Approximately 8,000 students took the first SAT® in 1926; that number has now climbed to two million students yearly.

But the SAT® does have competition from the ACT®, which was created in 1959 for basically the same purposes. While students throughout the U.S. know they can choose whichever test they prefer, geography tends to play a major role in their decision.

In New Jersey, for example, more than 90% of students choose the SAT®, while fewer than 10% choose the ACT®, according to statistics from Niche.com. This ratio of 9 to 1, or even greater, in favor of the SAT® is also reported in Maine, New Hampshire, Vermont, Massachusetts, Rhode Island, Connecticut, New York, Pennsylvania, Delaware, Maryland, Washington D.C., and Virginia.

Local students find the SAT® to be a natural progression from the PSAT® which they typically take in the fall of both their sophomore and junior years. Also, students often find the SAT® to be an easier test as it covers fewer subjects and gives students more time per question than does the ACT®.

States where students favor the ACT® are Alabama, Arkansas, Kansas, Kentucky, Louisiana, Mississippi, and Tennessee. But almost every college in the U.S. will accept either SAT® or ACT® scores, and no college requires both. So, what's the difference?

The material covered on both exams has a great deal of overlap. Both the SAT® and ACT® test students on critical reading skills, grammar and punctuation skills (referred to as "Writing" on the SAT® and "English" on the ACT®), and Math. While the SAT® provides students with a box of math formulas to refer to, the ACT® does not. Also, the ACT® has a science section as well as an optional essay, which may be eliminated in the future.

The scoring scale for the SAT® and ACT® varies greatly. The SAT® is scored on a scale ranging from 200 to 800 for each area of the test, while the ACT® is scored on a scale ranging from 0 to 36 for each area. According to the ACT® website, improving by just a single test point can be worth thousands of dollars in financial aid for one's college education. While not stated so succinctly, increased SAT® scores likewise boost a student's expected scholarship offers.

Since both are marked on a curve, students are basically competing with their peers when taking either test. So, the key is preparation. Standardized test scores are the main criteria that colleges use when allocating scholarship money, as it's the fairest way to compare students from a wide range of backgrounds and educational experiences. By improving their SAT® or ACT® scores, students can significantly increase their chances of being awarded scholarship money. Whatever money they are awarded for freshman year typically gets renewed for each of the student's subsequent three years of college. For example, an extra $8,000 merit award – due to higher SAT® or ACT® scores – ultimately becomes $32,000 of scholarship money.

The best strategy for college-bound students is to choose one exam to take – either the SAT® or ACT® – and devote some serious time and effort to preparation. The payoff could be substantial.

# What About Test Optional Colleges?

Among the multitude of lifestyle changes brought on by Covid was the opportunity to apply to colleges without SAT® scores – known as going "test optional." Colleges adopted this policy as a lifeline to ensure that they continued to receive applications from many more prospective students than they could possibly admit, maintaining their competitive reputation.

But the tide has turned, and current high school students who opt out of preparing for, and taking, the SAT® are greatly limiting their options. The SAT® (or ACT®) is once again required by many of the most elite, and competitive, universities throughout the country including Massachusetts Institute of Technology (MIT), Georgetown University, Georgia Tech and the University of Georgia, University of Florida and Florida State University, and the United States Naval Academy, Military Academy, and Air Force Academy. Colleges realize that no student is currently prevented from taking the SAT® due to Covid, so those who do not submit scores either did not bother taking the test or did not earn scores worth submitting.

Earning high SAT® scores is often the easiest way to impress college admissions officers. Applicants who go test optional may attract increased scrutiny on other materials, such as GPA, essays, extracurricular activities, and letters of recommendation, according to *Forbes*.

Also, many colleges and universities throughout the country that say they are "test optional" actually require test scores for out-of-state applicants. Others require test scores for students seeking enrollment in certain programs, particularly in the field of science. Students with low grade point averages (GPA) are often required to submit SAT® or ACT® scores to test optional colleges.

Most colleges will consider test scores, if submitted, with the exception of UCLA, UC-Berkeley, and others under the auspices of the University of California, which are "test blind."

College admissions officers who report being "holistic" consider all aspects of a student's application. It's safest for high school students to take the SAT® and then, when deciding whether to submit their results, compare them with the median scores of those accepted to a particular college. Students should access *Naviance*, or whichever software program their high school is using, to compare their SAT® scores with those of their peers who were accepted, or rejected, by a potential college.

SAT® scores often serve additional purposes, such as allowing students to opt out of placement tests prior to the start of their freshman year. Without SAT® scores, students who score poorly on placement tests are required to take non-credit "remedial" courses, typically in English and Math. They end up paying full college tuition and doing the required coursework, while not making any progress toward earning a degree. This typically lengthens the number of semesters required to graduate.

SAT® scores are also used by many colleges and scholarship programs to award grants (money that does not get paid back) to college-bound students. Later on, a student's SAT® scores are sometimes requested when applying for college internships, graduate school, and jobs. The SAT® is the one level playing field on which to compare all applicants and award those who have risen to the top.

Students who are still convinced that test optional is the way to go should consult the website fairtest.org for the latest list on test optional colleges and universities.

# Don't Forget About AP® Exams

The highest level of courses offered in high school are Advanced Placement (AP®) courses. They are offered in a wide variety of more than 30 academic subjects, including Studio Arts, Music Theory, Psychology, Micro and Macro Economics, Government and Politics, Calculus, Statistics, Biology, Chemistry, Physics, U.S. and World History, and many foreign languages, including Chinese, Japanese, Spanish, French, German and Italian. Not every high school offers the full roster of AP courses, and some high schools do not offer any at all.

The good news about AP® courses is that they give students an opportunity to do college level work while still in high school. Towards the end of the school year, in early May, students can take AP® exams which are written by College Board – the same company that offers the PSAT® and SAT®. AP® exams are typically about three hours long, and students are graded on a scale of 1 to 5. Students who score a 5 or 4 are frequently offered college credit. Some colleges even offer credit for an AP® score of 3.

In a recent year, nearly 1.2 million students took more than 4 million AP® exams in public high schools in the US, according to the College Board. Parents and students often ask, "Are AP courses really necessary?" The answer is both yes and no, depending on a student's ambitions and college goals. When students apply to college, they are basically in competition with their peers. Most colleges want a geographically well-rounded student body. So, college admissions officers compare all their applicants from the same high school and favor those with the most impressive academic record based on SAT® scores, GPA, and competitive course load. While there is no college in the country that outwardly states a requirement for AP® courses, students are well aware that these higher-level courses, that indicate an ability to successfully complete college level work, are viewed most favorably by college admission staff.

According to a report by NJ Spotlight, 28 percent of New Jersey high school seniors pass (with a score of 3 or higher) one or more AP® exams by the time they graduate. But locally, the numbers tend to be much higher. Recently, at Montgomery High School, 68% of students took at least one AP® exam and enjoyed a 94% exam pass rate. Bridgewater-Raritan High School had 50% of their students participate in AP® testing with a 95% pass rate, and Hillsborough High School had 44% of their students testing with an 89% exam pass rate.

Students who participate in the AP® program take, on average, three courses during their high school years. The most popular are English Language & Composition, U.S. History, English Literature & Composition, U.S. Government & Politics, World History, Psychology, and Calculus AB. Of course, there are some students who take ten or more exams. This may allow them to complete a year of college before ever stepping foot on campus. These students are definitely raising the bar for their classmates, making AP® courses increasingly popular with the college-bound crowd.

The bad news about AP® courses is that they can add additional stress to a student's high school experience. When high school students apply to competitive colleges, the criteria for acceptance includes consideration of how competitive a course load the students took. When a high school offers a vast number of AP® courses, top students often feel obliged to take as many of these courses as possible to be competitive with their peers with whom they may be vying for the same college seats.

Ideally, students who are academically prepared to do college level work should choose AP® courses in subjects compatible with their college plans. In other words, students planning to enter the medical field might take AP® Biology and/or AP® Chemistry. Students with hopes of becoming engineers or architects might favor AP® Calculus. Students who are considering a college major in Psychology or Economics would do well to take the coinciding

AP® course in high school to confirm their talent for, and interest in, the field.

Students who take several AP® courses during their high school years, and are successful on their AP® exams, should take note of which colleges offer credit for the courses. Most colleges do offer credit, but some do not. By attending a college that gives credit for high scoring AP® exams, students have greater opportunities to take additional courses. This often allows them to double major, take a major and a minor, or even graduate a semester or year early.

# Part III. Finding the Ideal College

# New Jersey's "Brain Drain"

New Jersey is known for its "brain drain" – with about 30,000 high school graduates heading out of state for college each year, leaving behind about 25,000 to attend in-state colleges and universities, according to Federal data. These statistics make New Jersey one of the top exporters of students. While more than half of all college-bound students leave our state – they don't go far!

Where do migrating students go? The Chronicle of Higher Education found that the vast majority of students are attracted to schools in nearby states. In a recent year, The University of Delaware was the most popular, enrolling 895 N.J. students. Penn State came in second, enrolling 884 N.J. students, and Drexel (in Philadelphia, PA) came in third, enrolling 631 students from the Garden State.

New York University was the fourth most popular, enrolling some 600 N.J. students, followed by three Philadelphia area schools: Villanova, Temple, and St. Joseph's University.

The top ten were rounded out with Syracuse (NY), Lehigh (PA) and the University of Maryland at College Park.

It's not that New Jersey is lacking colleges. It houses 19 public community colleges where many high school graduates choose to begin their education and strive to earn an associate degree without accumulating substantial student debt. New Jersey is also home to 11 public four-year colleges and universities, with highly regarded Rutgers University enrolling about 65,000 students spread over campuses in New Brunswick, Piscataway, Newark, and Camden. Also, New Jersey boasts 15 private colleges and universities, including Princeton University, which is often ranked as the premier college in the country, and Seton Hall University and Fairleigh Dickinson University, which are the state's largest.

Why does this brain drain exist? New Jersey is a small state, making it easy for students to cross the border to attend college while remaining close to home. New Jersey is also an expensive state. The high cost of attending college in New Jersey -- even the public universities -- makes out-of-state schools extremely attractive when they offer substantial scholarship funds.

Colleges in neighboring states actively recruit New Jersey students because they view New Jersey as having many stellar high schools and strong applicants. Colleges and universities that round out the list of "Top 25 schools with the most NJ students" are: Towson (MD), University of Rhode Island, University of Scranton (PA), James Madison (VA), Boston University (MA), University of Pittsburgh (PA), University of Michigan, Cornell University (NY), George Washington University (Washington D.C.), Pace University (NY), Johnson & Wales University (RI), Quinnipiac University (CT), West Chester University (PA), Northeastern University (MA), and Loyola University (MD).

# Benefits of Attending College In-State

One of the main advantages for New Jersey students to attend college in-state is a financial benefit. Students who rank in the top 15 percent of their high school class, at the end of either junior or senior year, may be eligible for the NJ Stars program. This covers the cost of tuition at all of New Jersey's 19 community colleges for up to five semesters, as long as students maintain a grade point average of 3.0 or higher. This program offers students the opportunity to earn their associate's degree without taking on college debt.

The NJ Stars II program is a continuation of the NJ Stars program. It provides students who successfully earned their associate's degree with a 3.25 grade point average or higher with funding to transfer to a New Jersey four year college or university to seek a bachelor's degree. NJ Stars II students are eligible for up to $2,500 annually.

Even students who do not participate in the New Jersey Stars program benefit financially by being entitled to pay the discounted "in-state" tuition and fees rate at any of New Jersey's 11 public four-year colleges and universities. The discount is substantial! For example, annual out-of-state tuition and fees at Rutgers University - New Brunswick is currently $33,963 as opposed to in-state tuition and fees of $16,263. Similarly, annual out-of-state tuition and fees at The College of New Jersey is currently $30,774 as opposed to in-state tuition and fees of $17,980.

Students who flee New Jersey to attend The University of Delaware are billed at the annual out-of-state tuition and fees rate of $37,930 rather than the in-state rate of $15,410. The same is true at the very popular Penn State-University Park where annual out-of-state tuition and fees is $36,476 compared to the in-state rate of $18,898. It often makes sense, from a financial point of view, for New Jersey students to seek the benefits of higher education right here in the Garden State.

# Research Is Key

While it's extremely valuable to know which colleges are popular with New Jersey students, both in and out of state, it's vital for all families to do their own research. A college investment is one of the largest expenses that most families will face in their lifetime. So, the key is to do some serious homework to identify best-fit colleges where students can prepare for the careers of their dreams at a college that meets their academic and social preferences.

College Board's *BigFuture* website offers a free college search feature that is an ideal place for families to start their research. There they will find a college search database with information on more than 2,400 four-year colleges in the U.S. As students select the specific criteria that are important to them, such as school size, location, availability of on-campus housing, choice of major, etc., the list of appropriate colleges starts to shrink. For example, if a student clicks on "location" and chooses New Jersey, Delaware and Pennsylvania as options, the list shrinks to 191 potential colleges. If the student then clicks "majors" and indicates that he/she is seeking Business and Management, the list reduces to 153 good-fit colleges. If the student then identifies a preference for an urban setting, the list further narrows to 31 colleges. Without leaving their computer, students can vastly narrow down the list of colleges worthy of further investigation. These colleges can be identified as reach, match, and safety schools by inputting one's SAT® scores and GPA. Further details are provided indicating the likelihood of admission, the range of SAT® scores for admitted students, graduation rate, and average annual cost of attendance after financial aid.

Parents and students should gather the facts on the real cost of attending any college under consideration. By googling the college name and COA (cost of attendance), one will find a breakdown of all the costs: tuition, fees, room and board, books, travel allocation, personal items allocation. Afterwards, one should google the particular college name and *net price calculator* to find the amount the average student pays to attend the institution for an academic year *after* subtracting scholarships and grants (which do not get paid back). This will best reflect the true cost of attendance.

At times, a particularly prestigious college is worth the investment, if you can gain acceptance. A "back door" way to get a degree from Columbia University, for those interested in engineering, is to gain acceptance to any of 100 other colleges – many of which aren't nearly as competitive – and enroll in the Combined Plan Program. Students spend three years at their college of choice and then transfer to Columbia for two years – earning a liberal arts bachelor's degree from the first school and an engineering bachelor's degree from Columbia.  This is a fabulous way for an average to above average student to earn an Ivy League degree, as Columbia's regular acceptance rate is only 3.9%.

Sometimes, in addition to seeking a college with a particular field of study, students are looking for a place with some very specific amenities. Students with a passion for golf, for example, might want to check out the University of Georgia where the golf course is consistently ranked among the top in the nation.  Other colleges and universities with truly impressive golf courses include Duke, Texas Tech, Stanford, University of Wisconsin, Virginia Tech, University of Virginia, Penn State, Yale, Clemson, Notre Dame, and Ohio State.

Students who are avid skiers might look towards Dartmouth College, which has sent student skiers to the Winter Olympics in past years. Other attractive options include University of Vermont and University of Colorado at Boulder.

Students with a passion for the arts would be enthralled by options at Oberlin. At this Ohio college, students can rent (at a cost of $5) famous works of art to adorn their dorm rooms.  Choices include paintings by Pablo Picasso and Henri de Toulouse-Lautrec. If music is a passion, students have access to 230 Steinway grand pianos – including one in every residence hall.

If it's all about food, a little research will let students know their options. James Madison University hosts many of the most popular fast-food chains, including Chick-Fila, Qdoba, Steak 'n Shake and Starbucks. At University of Massachusetts - Amherst, the largest collegiate dining service program in the U.S. reportedly creates 4,000 sushi rolls each day. Food trucks abound at several Philadelphia institutions: Drexel, La Salle, Temple, and University of Pennsylvania. If the preference is fine dining, High Point University in N.C. boasts of its "1924 Prime Steakhouse" where students can enjoy a weekly five-course meal in an upscale restaurant setting.

Some students are particularly attracted to colleges in a certain geographic setting. There are campuses that are waterfront: Eckerd College in Florida, Texas A & M, University of California – San Diego, University of Hawaii at Manoa. Others are nestled in mountain ranges: Washington and Lee University in Virginia, University of North Carolina–Ashville, Dartmouth College in New Hampshire, Bates College in Maine. Still others are center stage in the midst of thriving urban environments: New York University, University of Pennsylvania in Philadelphia, University of Southern California in Los Angeles, Georgetown in our nation's capital.

Once a list of preferred colleges has been developed, students should carefully examine the website of each of these schools. Then, for more objective information, they should refer to the latest issue of U.S. News & World Report's *Best Colleges*. This annual magazine ranks colleges and offers a great deal of helpful information about each college in the U.S. including acceptance rate, average SAT® scores, diversity of students, average size of classes, most popular majors, and retention rate (the percent of students who return for their sophomore year). Retention rate is an excellent indicator of how happy students are with the quality of any college or university.

Students with aspirations of working for a particular company should find out which colleges they recruit at for interns and for full time employees. Many firms favor graduates from specific colleges and universities.

Comparing statistics can be extremely helpful, even among colleges right here in the Garden State. New Jersey boasts 28 four-year institutions of higher education, each with its own strengths and attractions. The College of New Jersey (TCNJ) is currently among the top five Regional Universities – North, according to *U.S. News and World Report*. It boasts a 90% freshmen retention rate and 42% of its classes have fewer than 20 students.

In the category of Best National Universities, Rutgers University-New Brunswick recently ranked #40 while Stevens Institute of Technology ranked #76. Their freshmen retention rates are 92% and 93%, respectively. Rutgers offers a selection of more than 150 majors and minors, making it attractive to students who have not yet chosen a career path. Stevens Institute is highly regarded for its stellar education in fields of engineering, with its most popular majors including mechanical, civil, electrical, and chemical engineering. Since students are also concerned about their likelihood of securing gainful employment in their field of study after graduation, *U.S. News & World Report* now includes postgraduate salary information on 1,000 schools.

Of course, a key criterion in choosing a college should be to get the best value possible for your tuition dollars. *Money* also releases annual rankings. It takes into consideration educational quality, affordability, and alumni earnings. *Money* includes a "value added" grade based on how well students typically perform at particular colleges vs. what would be expected based on their economic and academic backgrounds. *Money* screens out any colleges with graduation rates below the median as well as those facing financial difficulties.

Typically, students worry about their chances of getting accepted to an impressive college or university. A little research, here too, can help put into perspective the likelihood of meeting with success. *Money* publishes a list of "The 50 Best Colleges You Can Actually Get Into." These schools, which all accept more than 50% of their applicants, include many that are popular with New Jersey students: Rutgers University – New Brunswick, James Madison University, Ohio State University, University of Illinois Urbana-Champaign, Indiana University – Bloomington, University of Wisconsin – Madison, Texas A & M, University of Pittsburgh, Purdue University, University of Massachusetts – Amherst, Virginia Tech, University of Delaware, Manhattan College, Clemson University, and Massachusetts Maritime Academy.

Once students and parents are armed with all the information they can find about their colleges of interest, it's time to attend college fairs. These take place at many high schools throughout New Jersey and admission is always free. Typically, representatives from more than 100 colleges, universities, technical schools, and the military host tables filled with materials and are happy to answer individual questions. These local fairs provide the perfect opportunity for "one stop shopping" to gather materials and answers to all college-related questions.

There are also national college fairs, including one typically held in March at the New Jersey Convention and Exposition Center, where students can meet with representatives from more than 300 colleges. The grand scope of this event provides opportunities for students to attend workshops on a multitude of topics: College Search Process, How to Write a Great College Essay, College Athletics, Performing Arts, Applying to Health Professions, and Financial Aid and Scholarships.

To make the most of these opportunities, students should do their homework in advance. They should make a list of the colleges in which they are interested, and the questions to which they are seeking answers. Then, while talking to college representatives, students should ask for a business card. Once home, students should email the reps of colleges in which they are particularly interested, thanking them for their time and information, and expressing interest in their school. This is the basis of establishing a relationship with the college rep who is often the very same person who will be making the decision as to whom is accepted or rejected from the school.

# Touring Colleges

There's nothing quite like touring the grounds of a college campus and experiencing, first-hand, what the school has to offer. But with more than 4,000 two and four-year colleges in the U.S., and more than 600 colleges within 200 miles of Central New Jersey, students should narrow down their search to potential "good fit colleges" before embarking on their road trips.

Visiting a college when classes are in session allows high school students to take in the atmosphere and to visualize what it would be like to be a part of the student body. New Jersey students should utilize the days they are off from school, which are not college holidays, to schedule these tours. Columbus Day, Election Day, the November Teacher Convention days (in many New Jersey school districts) and Presidents' Day often provide perfect opportunities to investigate, first-hand, colleges of interest.

Spring break is typically another perfect opportunity for high school students to tour college campuses while classes, activities, and college life are in full swing. Colleges tend to schedule their spring breaks in early March, while high schools hold them in late March or April. So, it's an ideal time for high school students to visit colleges and start to identify which ones may, or may not, be potential "good fit" schools.

If parents are available during a student's spring break, it's a perfect time for a road trip to visit out-of-town colleges. The vast majority of students attend college within five hours of home, so the destination does *not* need to be a far-off locale. If a student dreams of attending a big city school, then a tour of colleges in the Boston or Washington D.C. areas may prove fruitful. If a student prefers a suburban or rural environment, then a drive through Pennsylvania offers an option of touring close to 100 different colleges and universities.

Students who are on their own during spring break can still put the week to great use. By visiting two of New Jersey's highly ranked schools, The College of New Jersey (TCNJ) and Rutgers University, students can quickly come to the realization of the type of college they prefer.

TCNJ hosts about 7,000 students on a tranquil, suburban campus of 289 acres. The school's most popular majors are Teacher Education, Business, and Biological Sciences, and most classes have 25 or fewer students.

Rutgers University in New Brunswick is home to about 35,000 students in a distinctly urban setting. The list of majors is almost limitless, and class size can exceed 300 students.

Students visiting both schools seldom like them equally. They usually find themselves drawn to one atmosphere over the other and can use this self-awareness in choosing other colleges to visit in the future. For example, students who like TCNJ often find Villanova and Lehigh to be appealing. Those who prefer Rutgers often look favorably upon Penn State and New York University (NYU).

The most important aspect of a college visit is the official tour. It's important for students to contact colleges ahead of time to schedule their campus tour which is usually offered every weekday, both in the morning and the afternoon. Students should register in advance for a specific tour, and then be sure to sign in when they arrive on the day of their visit. The reason this is vital is that colleges track student interest. When reviewing college applications, admissions officers often check to see if the student has visited the campus – an indication that the student is a serious applicant. When students live within a few hours of a college, and do not visit prior to filing an application, the admissions team often interprets this as a lack of real interest in the school. College admissions personnel favor students whom they believe will likely attend their school, if offered the chance to do so.

Students should take notes during their college tours. At the time of each tour, students think they will remember exactly what they are seeing and being told. But problems arise after students have visited several colleges and start mixing up the details of the various schools.

When students later get to work on their college applications, they should personalize each one by emphasizing the qualities that most attract them to each particular college. This is where the notes they took during their tours come in very handy. Was there a particular major that appealed to them? Are there enticing internship opportunities? Is there a study abroad program in an exotic location that would tie in well with a particular course of study? By personalizing each application, students gain an impressive advantage in the competitive college application process. Admissions people strongly favor students who have done their homework and know exactly where they want to spend their college years.

As for the college tours, most originate at the Campus Center, which typically houses the main cafeteria, or food court, as well as the bookstore and a host of amenities. Students with strong dietary preferences or restrictions (vegan, vegetarian, kosher, gluten-free) should pay particular attention to the culinary offerings, as the campus dining facility would provide them with most of their college meals. Other attractions found here may include cinemas, bowling alleys, pool, ping-pong and air hockey tables, climbing walls, scores of high-definition televisions, coffee bars, convenience stores, banks, beauty salons, meeting rooms, and study lounges.

Continuing on to the athletic facilities, most college tours will highlight their stadiums and gymnasiums, but some offer so much more. Top athletic colleges often feature such amenities as underground practice fields, ice hockey and skating arenas, hydrotherapy pools, saunas, rehabilitation facilities, and theaters for press conferences. For student athletes, such luxuries can serve as a big draw.

Moving on to the more academic-oriented facilities, many colleges feature impressive museums in the fields of art, natural history, anthropology, and natural science. Other colleges host state-of-the-art engineering laboratories in areas such as biomedical engineering, digital signal processing, and robotics and intelligent systems. There are also colleges that are medically oriented with simulation laboratories that give students hands-on clinical experience. These labs feature rooms occupied by high-tech mannequins that simulate symptoms, diseases, and conditions that future doctors are likely to face in hospitals. The "maternity room" at Penn State University even features a mannequin that gives birth (to a baby mannequin).

After students tour a campus, eat in the dining hall, visit the Campus Center, observe all the amenities, and chat with current students, it's usually crystal clear whether or not it's a place they'd like to call home for the next four years.

# Pay Attention to Graduation Rates

"What is your four-year graduation rate?" This may be one of the most important questions that college-bound students and their parents can ask when considering a potential college. An article in *Money* stated, "the failure to graduate students in four years has become so commonplace that schools are now showing you their six-year graduation rate." Unfortunately, that fact is usually not very evident.

The "Best Colleges" Guide by *U.S. News & World Report*, considered a top resource of college information, lists the graduation rate as one of its key criteria in ranking hundreds of colleges and universities. Readers may assume it indicates a four-year graduation rate, but it's actually a six-year graduation rate.

A government website that provides a great deal of extremely helpful information to college-bound students and their parents is collegescorecard.ed.gov. One key category, addressing the graduation rate at U.S. colleges and universities, states, "The graduation rate for degree granting schools is the proportion of entering students that graduated at this school within 8 years of entry…" Students and parents who are budgeting for a college diploma need to know, in advance, whether to multiply the annual cost of attendance (including tuition, room, board, books and fees) by four or six or even eight!

Sometimes there's a good reason for students to take additional years to earn a diploma. Perhaps they switched majors and many of their credits did not carry over to their new course of study. On the other hand, perhaps it was out of their control. Maybe some of their required courses were not readily available, requiring a longer college stay to meet graduation requirements.

Of course, there are some universities that boast impressive four-year graduation rates of 90% or higher for their undergraduate student body, including University of Notre Dame, Washington and Lee University, University of Virginia, Georgetown University, Duke University, Babson College, Swarthmore College, and Tufts University.

According to U.S. News & World Report, other than Princeton University, which has a four-year graduation rate of 88%, the only New Jersey colleges or universities with four-year graduation rates at or above 60% are The College of New Jersey (75%), Rutgers University – New Brunswick (70%), Seton Hall University (66%), Drew University (64%), Stockton University (62%), Rider University and Caldwell University (61%), and Ramapo College of New Jersey and Monmouth University (60%).

Another enlightening question that students and parents should ask of college administrators at any school under consideration is, "How many of your graduates are either employed or enrolled in graduate school within six months of graduation and/or within a year?" Every college and university is required by law to keep these statistics and make them available.

Prospective students should also ask colleges whether on-campus housing is guaranteed for four years, or whether upper classmen need to seek housing off-campus. They should also inquire about food options, especially if they have dietary restrictions, to find out if there would be a large selection of healthy options for their culinary needs and preferences.

If students are hoping to participate in a particular program (such as study abroad in a preferred country), or a favorite sport, they should inquire about the likelihood of being able to do so at any college under consideration.

Asking the right questions can be crucial to making an educated decision on the next step of one's academic and career life.

# Predict Future with "College Scorecard"

Ten years ago, the federal government created *College Scorecard* to be used as a type of *Consumer Reports* for colleges. Ever since, data has been collected on colleges throughout the U.S. regarding the cost of attending, graduation rates, and actual salaries that alumni were earning, based on specific degrees, four years after graduation. Numbers don't lie, so students and parents can now enter the college process wide-eyed, able to compare the cost of earning a particular degree at a specific college with the salary that its alumni are earning early in their careers.

The website featuring this information is collegescorecard.ed.gov. By typing in *Rutgers*, for example, and then choosing the New Brunswick campus and bachelor's degree, data appears showing that the graduation rate (within 8 years of entering the school) is 83% with an average annual cost of $15,000. By clicking Rutgers University – New Brunswick, and expanding "Fields of Study," one can access the median earnings of alumni sorted by major four years after graduation. By choosing Rutgers graduates with a degree in Computer and Information Sciences, for example, you will find current median earnings of $114,399 four years after getting their bachelor's degree, while those with a degree in Psychology were earning a median salary of $49,641.

Another way to use the College Scorecard is to search by "Fields of Study" and select a major. By choosing Economics, for example, the names of 804 colleges appear that offer a bachelor's degree in this field. In sorting by earnings, Duke University currently tops the list with median earnings, four years after graduation, of $153,139. Students with a degree from Harvard can expect $124,570, Boston College $93,934, Villanova $88,087, NYU $87,957, Drexel $83,676, Rutgers – New Brunswick $78,565, Penn State $75,421, University of Maryland $72,814, and The College of New Jersey $67,369.

These schools have vastly different acceptance rates, costs of attendance, and graduation rates. But the numbers are available, allowing all college-bound students and their families to make educated choices on one of the most impactful financial and social decisions of their lives.

# 5 Latest Trends in College Admissions Process

Students about to embark on the ever-challenging college application process would do well to know the latest trends and use this knowledge to their benefit.

1) The volume of college applications has continued its upward spiral. More students are applying to college than ever before, and they are applying to a greater number of schools. The Common Application reports the overall volume of college applications increased by 30% over the past three years.

   New York University (NYU), for example, received 120,000 applications from high school students graduating this year, and 85,000 applications from those who graduated in 2020 – an increase of 41%. As a result, the acceptance rate has fallen to record lows at many of the most sought-after universities.

2) Tuition and fees have also continued to rise. Over the past 20 years, costs for in-state students to attend public universities increased by 175%, while costs to attend private national universities increased by 134%, according to *Forbes*. Colleges and universities with a sticker price exceeding $80,000 per year (including tuition, fees, room, and board) include University of Pennsylvania, Boston College, Cornell University, Franklin & Marshall College, Tufts University, Brown University, Amherst College, Wake Forest University, and the University of Southern California. The exact figures can be found in U.S. News & World Report's *Best Colleges*.

3) More students are recognizing the benefit of applying Early Decision (ED) and/or Early Action (EA) to colleges, typically requiring that applications be submitted by November 1st of senior year. Many colleges report a significantly higher acceptance rate for ED and EA applicants.

At Williams College in Massachusetts (ranked #1 National Liberal Arts College in *Best Colleges*), the Early Decision acceptance rate is 40% while the regular acceptance rate is 9%. The same numbers are reported for #2 ranked Amherst College, also in Massachusetts, according to statistics from *Niche.com*.

4) Acceptance into direct entry medical programs, where students move seamlessly from their undergraduate education into medical school, has become increasingly competitive. Such programs are offered at many schools, including Rutgers and Rowan universities in New Jersey, and Drexel, Temple, Thomas Jefferson, and University of Pittsburgh in Pennsylvania. At many of these programs, the acceptance rate ranges from 1% to 5%.

5) Ever since The College Board stopped offering SAT Subject Tests (also known as SAT II exams) in 2021, college admissions officers have placed a greater importance on Advanced Placement courses and the scores students are earning on these end-of-year exams. Enrollment in AP® courses is quite popular in Central New Jersey, as students seek to stand out, academically, among their peers.

# Public Ivies vs. Original Eight

When considering the most prestigious colleges in the United States, the eight Ivy League schools, all located in the northeast, most often come to mind. The first of these elite schools was Harvard, founded in 1636, with Yale following in 1702. Five more of these institutions were established in the mid-1700's (University of Pennsylvania, Princeton, Brown, Columbia, and Dartmouth) while Cornell was founded in 1865.

But the term *Ivy League* wasn't coined until 1954 when the NCAA athletic conference for Division I was formed. Since then, these elite schools have certainly maintained their athletic rivalries. But a sense of academic competitiveness thrives as well, with many of these institutions claiming bragging rights for the number of U.S. presidents they've educated. Harvard: John Adams, John Quincy Adams, Rutherford B. Hayes, Theodore Roosevelt, Franklin D. Roosevelt, John F. Kennedy, George W. Bush, Barack Obama. Yale: William Howard Taft, George H.W. Bush, Bill Clinton, George W. Bush. Columbia: Theodore Roosevelt, Franklin D. Roosevelt, Barack Obama. Princeton: James Madison, Woodrow Wilson. University of Pennsylvania: William Henry Harrison, Donald Trump. (Several presidents attended more than one school.)

Decades later, the phrase "Public Ivy" was coined. It was first used by author Richard Moll in his 1985 book, "*Public Ivies: A Guide to America's Best Public Undergraduate Colleges and Universities.*" He named eight public universities where students could get a top-notch education for a fraction of the cost of their prestigious private counterparts: College of William and Mary (VA), Miami University (OH), University of California, University of Michigan, University of North Carolina–Chapel Hill, University of Texas–Austin, University of Vermont, University of Virginia.

Close to 40 years later, some of these same institutions still head the list of *Top Public National Universities*, according to the 2024 edition of "Best Colleges" by *U.S. News and World Report.* Its rankings top the list with University of California (Berkeley and Los Angeles), University of Michigan, University of North Carolina – Chapel Hill, University of Virginia, University of Florida and University of California at Davis and San Diego, University of Texas at Austin, and Georgia Institute of Technology and University of California at Irvine.

Students who pay full price, without need-based or merit aid, often find that the annual cost of attending a prestigious in-state public university is tens of thousands of dollars less than that of attending an Ivy League institution. For example, recent costs for in-state students, including room and board, at University of California – Los Angeles totaled $31,035, while the fees at Harvard added up to $76,763.

It's wise for students to compare all aspects of potential colleges, including academic reputations and financial commitments, before making their big decision.

# Choosing a College Major

The billionaire investor Mark Cuban, who attained celebrity status for his role on the highly rated ABC-TV show *Shark Tank*, garnered a great deal of attention for views he expressed at the NBA All-Star Technology Summit. (Cuban is the owner of the Dallas Mavericks basketball team.)

Cuban warned that millions of jobs are at risk of becoming automated in coming years and feared that even people with in-demand skills, such as computer coding, could soon be displaced. Citing "the automation of automation," Cuban said that computers could soon learn how to write software better than humans. His advice to college-bound students is to major in the liberal arts. "The nature of jobs is changing," said Cuban, who recommended Philosophy, English, and foreign languages as some of the majors that will do well in the future job market. Cuban believes that people with "soft skills," such as creative thinking, adaptability, and communication, will have the advantage in an automated workplace.

This advice differs from that offered by the online job-posting site *Indeed*, which listed eleven college majors with high earning potential: Economics, Nursing, Architecture, Accounting, Physical Sciences (Biology, Chemistry and Physics), Computer Science, Mechanical Engineering, Business Administration, Psychology, International Relations, and Aerospace Engineering.

College-bound students need to consider both the high-compensation fields of today, and the likely scenario of the job market of the future, when choosing their course of study. They should carefully consider all the ramifications of their potential major before starting college, as it's preferable to enter college with a chosen major, rather than "undecided." The reasons for this revolve around both time and money.

Students who enter college "undecided," or who change their major after beginning their studies, frequently end up spending more than four years at their college in order to meet the graduation requirements of their major. Also, when students begin their college studies "undecided," they later must apply to be admitted to the department of their choice. There is no guarantee that they will be accepted. So, once students decide they want to be business majors, for example, if they are not admitted to the College of Business, they must either change their career path or transfer to a different college.

College Board's *BigFuture* website offers a free 60 question career quiz with the aim of matching one's passions and interests with ideal occupations. Details for matched careers are provided including projected job growth, most common education level, and median yearly income.

Students who start college with a chosen major and a clear career path can often cut years of education, a great deal of stress, and a substantial amount of money, from their higher education experience.

Many colleges offer direct entry and dual degree programs whereby students move right into a master's program upon completing their undergraduate (bachelor's) education. Direct entry programs are particularly attractive in that students do not have to take entrance exams, eliminating the stressful process of preparing for, and taking, standardized tests. Basically, if they meet certain requirements during their undergraduate years, they move right into the advanced degree program in their chosen field.

These programs are particularly popular in the medical field with combined programs offered for those seeking to become doctors, physician assistants, and physical therapists. While some combined programs, particularly those preparing students to become doctors, often take the traditional eight years, others are completed after five or six years.

Drexel University, for example, offers an eight-year BA/BS+MD Early Assurance program that allows students to gain early acceptance into both their undergraduate major and medical school at the same time. The program is open to students majoring in Biological Sciences, Chemistry, or Biomedical Engineering.

Students hoping to complete both college and medical school in seven years should look towards The College of New Jersey (TCNJ) or Penn State. TCNJ offers a seven-year accelerated BS/MD program with New Jersey Medical School. Similarly, Penn State offers a seven-year accelerated program with Thomas Jefferson University in Philadelphia.

There are also combined seven and eight year programs between New Jersey Medical School and several New Jersey schools: Caldwell University, Drew University, Montclair State University, New Jersey Institute of Technology, The College of New Jersey, Rutgers University, and Stevens Institute of Technology. This program does require students to take the MCAT and meet other stringent qualifications.

Students seeking to become physical therapists often seek combined six-year programs. Popular schools offering this option include Northeastern, Seton Hall, LaSalle, Duquesne, Quinnipiac, University of the Sciences, Ithaca College, and Boston University.

Students looking to become Physician Assistants can reach their goal with a five-year, dual degree, program offered at a wide variety of colleges and universities. Those with direct entry programs in the NY/NJ/PA area include Albany College of Pharmacy and Health Sciences, Hofstra University, Stockton University, De Sales University, Gannon University, Duquesne University, Jefferson University, King's College, and Seton Hill University.

Students with a passion for business might seek a 4 + 1 program, combining their undergraduate degree with a Master's in Business Administration (MBA). This eliminates the need to take the GMAT exam and cuts one year off the typically two-year MBA experience. Popular schools offering this option include Fordham University, Penn State University, Fairfield University, Seton Hall University, University of Scranton, Quinnipiac University, and Drexel University.

Basically, students with a clearly defined career goal, a high GPA, and impressive SAT® scores, can head off to college knowing they will graduate with the highest degree needed for success in their chosen field.

Even students who are not looking far ahead, trying to tie their bachelor's degree to an advanced degree, can benefit greatly by having a sense of direction as they head to college. Not everyone is an A+ student with perfect SAT® scores. Students with less than stellar grades and test scores can particularly benefit by knowing the academic field they wish to pursue, as many extremely impressive colleges look for students who are the right match for their programs.

Maritime academies, for example, have recently earned accolades as their graduates attain among the highest-paying entry-level jobs. The acceptance rate at the Massachusetts Maritime Academy and the California Maritime Academy was 90% and 82%, respectively.

STEM (Science, Technology, Engineering and Math) graduates are likewise in high demand for well-paying jobs. Fortunately, some very prestigious colleges are more accessible than students imagine. Stonehill College, in Easton, MA, reports an 85% acceptance rate for early decision candidates and offers a "back door" into the prestigious University of Notre Dame. Students who major in engineering at Stonehill and maintain a "B" average for three years are guaranteed admission into Notre Dame for two years and are awarded both a Bachelor of Arts and a Bachelor of Science degree.

Another highly regarded "tech" school, Virginia Tech, has an acceptance rate of 56% and very competitive annual tuition rates of about $15,000 for in-state students and $36,000 for out-of-state students.

Students seeking a career in nursing would do well to consider Molloy College in Rockville Centre, NY. This Catholic college on Long Island, with an acceptance rate of over 75%, is consistently ranked among the best for its nursing curriculum.

# Lifetime Salaries Vary by Millions

As millions of students head off to college each fall, well-meaning parents often encourage them to choose the major of their dreams. Sometimes, students have known for years the particular career that would be perfect for them. Other times, students enter college "undecided" and end up making a decision as they move through their coursework. But few students realize the economic impact of their choices.

On average, an individual with a bachelor's degree earns $1.2 million more over their careers compared to peers with only a high school diploma. But not all majors are created equal.

From a monetary point of view, the choice of major can either launch a student into a high paying career or leave the graduate struggling to pay off skyrocketing student debt. In fact, college graduates with the highest-paying majors earn $3.4 million more than those with the lowest-paying majors, over the course of their careers, according to a study by the Georgetown University Center of Education and the Workforce.

The choice of major can have an even bigger impact on future earnings than choice of school, according to PayScale, an online salary, benefits, and compensation information company. So which majors reap the greatest reward for your tuition and time? Hands down, STEM majors. Statistics from *PayScale* listing salaries of professionals with ten years of experience, placed STEM careers in all top ten spots.

Petroleum Engineering took the top spot with an average salary of $212,500, ten years out. It's offered as a major at many campuses of Penn State University and at several Texas universities. Operations Research and Industrial Engineering, which came in 2nd at $191,800, is offered at Columbia and Cornell universities, University of Texas – Austin, and University of Massachusetts – Amherst.

Interaction Design, in 3$^{rd}$ place at $173,600, is offered at Carnegie Mellon, Purdue and Stanford universities, as well as Rochester Institute of Technology, University of Southern California, and University of California – San Diego.

The next seven highest paying fields, with average annual salaries ten years out, ranging from $164,000 to $157,800, were Applied Economics & Management, Building Science, Actuarial Mathematics, Operations Research, Systems Engineering, Optical Science & Engineering, and Information & Computer Science.

Of course, these are national statistics that do not take into account the various job climates in different parts of the country. In New Jersey, for example, the highest-paying industries include Pharmaceutical Research & Development and Pharmaceutical Manufacturing. The reason is simply that New Jersey is home to some of the world's largest pharmaceutical companies, including Novartis, Johnson & Johnson, Bristol-Myers Squibb, and Merck. Other high paying fields in the Garden State are Information Technology and Financial Services.

Perhaps students should take this information into account when they check off the "choice of major" box on their college applications!

# Top Return on Investment Colleges

Students searching for their ideal college often consider many criteria, including location, campus life, and academic options. But a key criterion that students should take into account is the college's ROI – return on investment – which identifies the long-term financial value of a degree.

With annual tuition and fees at some colleges exceeding $80,000, it's wise for students to consider what the likely payoff will be in terms of their future earnings. They can turn to research conducted by The Georgetown University Center on Education and the Workforce, which identified the ROI at 4,500 colleges throughout the United States.

A degree from the sixteen non-profit or public colleges/universities topping the list all had a 40-year ROI exceeding $2 million. These schools, starting with the highest ROI, are University of Health Sciences & Pharmacy in St. Louis (MO), Albany College of Pharmacy & Health Sciences (NY), MCPHS University (MA), California Institute of Technology, Massachusetts Institute of Technology, Harvey Mudd College (CA), Bentley University (MA), Babson College (MA), University of Pennsylvania, Stanford University (CA), Princeton University (NJ), Carnegie Mellon University (PA), University of the Sciences (PA), Stevens Institute of Technology (NJ), Georgetown University (DC), and Lehigh University (PA).

The 40-year ROI for New Jersey public and private non-profit institutions exceeded $2 million at both Princeton University and Stevens Institute of Technology, and 1.7 million at New Jersey Institute of Technology. Other New Jersey schools with a 40-year ROI exceeding $1.2 million, in decreasing order, are Rutgers University - Camden, Rutgers University – Newark, Seton Hall University, Rutgers University – New Brunswick, The College of New Jersey, Ramapo College, and Monmouth University.

It's wise for students to carefully consider their likely future earnings when taking on college debt. According to the U.S. Department of Education, 1.23 million New Jersey residents collectively hold $44.8 billion in federal student loans. By studying available data, such as that provided by The Georgetown University Center on Education and the Workforce, college-bound students can aim to make financially sound decisions.

# Universities That Produce Fortune 500 CEOs

If your goal is to become the Chief Executive Officer (CEO) of a Fortune 500 company, you may be wondering exactly where you should go to college. The truth is, there are many options.

*U.S. News & World Report* recently investigated the educational backgrounds of the top CEOs following the release of Fortune 500's list of companies with the highest revenue. It turns out that there's a great deal of diversity. In fact, none of the CEOs among the top 10 companies on the Fortune 500 list attended the same college. The President and CEO of Walmart, C. Douglas McMillon, earned his bachelor's degree from the University of Arkansas, while Berkshire Hathaway's CEO, Warren Buffett, graduated from the University of Nebraska (Lincoln). The colleges represented by the other eight top executives are Harvard, Texas A & M, Auburn University, University of Nottingham U.K., Boston College, Indian Institute of Technology, University of California (Santa Cruz) and University of Colorado (Boulder).

Common majors for these business tycoons include business administration, accounting, economics, and various fields of engineering, science, technology, and math. Top executives at the most prestigious companies, nationwide, represent a vast array of universities and majors.

# Part IV. Filing Successful College Applications

# Tips for Choosing "Good Fit" Colleges

The key to filing college applications that will attract letters of acceptance is to recognize what the colleges are seeking and then focus the applications accordingly. First and foremost, colleges seek students who are academically prepared to succeed and are motivated to maximize the opportunities offered by the college. A student's GPA is therefore important, since it demonstrates how the student has performed academically in a high school environment. SAT® or ACT® scores are also critical to many colleges, as they are considered to be a strong indication of a student's potential to succeed in a college academic environment. But by the time a student is filing college applications, the GPA and standardized test scores have usually been determined.

Another key criterion for college admissions officers is the determination of what a student will likely contribute to the college community. Is the student a top athlete, musician, or student with proven leadership abilities? Colleges seek depth of involvement rather than breadth, so students should focus their time and attention on a limited number of activities in which they excel. Colleges are not in the market for well-rounded people, but rather for those with an impressive record of accomplishment in a specific field. By accepting thousands of students who each excel in specific activities, colleges end up with a well-rounded student body.

Once students honestly assess what they have to offer a college community, and what they are seeking out of their college experience, they can choose schools that are a "good fit." Students in search of the perfect college are pretty much all looking for the same thing. First of all, they have to be able to gain acceptance to the college. Secondly, they need to succeed academically in college – hopefully cherishing the experience. Lastly, they must expect that, upon graduation, their field of study will put them on track for a well-paying career.

*Time* magazine went in search of colleges that fit the bill, choosing only colleges that accept at least 66% of applicants. Several colleges within a few hours of New Jersey made the list, including Molloy College, La Salle University, and three Jesuit Universities: St. Joseph's, Fairfield, and University of Scranton. All of these colleges also had a high "freshmen retention rate," which is the percent of freshmen that returned for their sophomore year. And the most popular majors, at all of these colleges, were in fields with high potential career earnings.

Molloy, a small college in Rockville Centre, NY, was also recognized by *USA Today* as the 4th best college in the U.S. at which to earn a nursing degree. It was topped only by Columbia University, NYU, and Georgetown, and ranked higher than the prestigious Johns Hopkins University! Its acceptance rate was 79% and retention rate was 87%. To top it off, 64% of its classes had fewer than 20 students and current annual tuition is $36,000.

La Salle and St. Joseph's are both popular Philadelphia-area colleges. La Salle reports its most popular majors as Registered Nursing, Marketing and Management, Psychology, Accounting, and Finance. La Salle has an 81% acceptance rate and 72% of its freshmen returned for their sophomore year.

St. Joseph's is best known for its business majors, including Marketing, Management, Accounting and Finance. Of the students who applied to St. Joseph's, 83% were accepted and 89% of its freshmen returned for their sophomore year.

Fairfield University, in the upscale town of Fairfield, CT, is home of the impressive Charles F. Dolan School of Business, School of Engineering, and Marion Peckham Egan School of Nursing and Health Studies. While this university has a regular acceptance rate of 56%, it rewards students who apply Early Decision with an 83% acceptance rate. The school's retention rate is 90%.

The University of Scranton in Pennsylvania is most popular for degrees in Biological Sciences, Registered Nursing and Business/Marketing. Applicants enjoy an overall acceptance rate of 80%, and 88% of freshmen return for their sophomore year.

Sometimes students seeking a particular type of education have more options than they realize. College-bound students seeking a Jesuit education, but lacking the stellar credentials required by the likes of Georgetown University and Boston College, have many opportunities. As discussed above, St. Joseph's University, Fairfield University, and The University of Scranton all accepted a majority of their applicants. Likewise, John Carroll and Xavier, Jesuit universities in Ohio, have acceptance rates of 88% and 84%, respectively.

The key, for most students, is to carefully identify the colleges that would be a good match for their talents and interests, and then effectively communicate this information to their colleges of choice. College admissions officers often look kindly upon students who are passionate about their institution and enthusiastic about a particular major that is offered.

While it's natural for high school students to worry about whether or not they will get accepted to their college of choice, they should realize that college admissions officers worry as well. Their concern is whether or not the students they accept will actually enroll. And their apprehension is well founded, as very few colleges in the U.S. enjoy a "yield" (percent of accepted students who actually enroll) of over 60%. Those that do include all eight Ivy League institutions as well as Barnard College, University of Notre Dame, and the University of Chicago.

Why is there such a gap between the number of students who are accepted and the number who actually enroll?

One reason is that a vast number of students are applying to a multitude of colleges. This is feasible due to the existence of the

"Common Application" – one application that is accepted by more than 1,000 colleges and universities, including some outside the U.S. Since students ultimately enroll at only one college, there are a lot of colleges taking a hit to their yield.

Another factor is the practice of students applying to one college "early decision" while simultaneously submitting applications to other colleges. If a student is accepted by the early decision college, he/she must decline all other acceptances.

Students can use this information to their benefit by showing demonstrated interest to the colleges to which they apply. Colleges all want to boast of the highest yield possible, so it benefits them to accept those students who appear most likely to attend. Students can put themselves in this desirable category by visiting college campuses and signing in, contacting college admissions officers with pertinent questions, and customizing their application essays to demonstrate interest for each particular college to which they are applying. A little personalized attention directed toward a college can help a student greatly increase the likelihood of receiving a letter of acceptance.

# Advantages of Early Action and Early Decision

Applying "early decision" dramatically increases a student's chance of gaining acceptance to most colleges and universities. The key is for students to do their homework early – researching and visiting colleges and identifying the one that would, hands down, be their top choice. The next step is to apply early decision, submitting the application by the early decision deadline (typically November 1st) and signing that you will attend that particular college if accepted.

Colleges are well aware that many students apply to ten or more colleges. But they have no way of knowing which students, if accepted, would actually attend their school. With multi-million dollar annual budgets, it's extremely beneficial for colleges to know which students, if accepted, would definitely be attending (and paying tuition, room, board, and fees). Since early decision applications are binding, guaranteeing that accepted students will attend, it's advantageous for colleges to favor these students. Admitting early decision students also greatly increases the college's yield.

Some highly respected colleges offer close to a 100% acceptance rate for students who apply early decision, including Alfred University in New York. Alfred offers a beautiful, friendly campus, small class sizes, and impressive programs in such fields as art, engineering, and equestrian studies. Early decision applicants enjoy a 98% acceptance rate, while regular applicants have a 51% acceptance rate.

Closer to home, Manhattan College, just a few minutes from the George Washington Bridge, offers a 93% acceptance rate to early decision applicants. This Catholic college, with Division I sports, boasts nationally accredited professional schools in Business, Education, Health, and Engineering. Its close proximity to Manhattan provides students with internship opportunities at such prestigious firms as CBS, General Electric, Merrill Lynch, J.P. Morgan, and The N.Y. Mets. Its overall acceptance rate is 75%.

For students ready to commit to one particular college, there are many top institutions that greatly increase the odds of acceptance for early decision applicants. The percentages of students accepted early decision, in comparison to regular decision, are: University of Pennsylvania 23% to 6%, Duke University 24% to 6%, New York University (NYU) 30% to 13%, College of the Holy Cross 73% to 43%, Providence College 84% to 58%, Ithaca College 93% to 78%, American University 85% to 64%, Dickinson College 71% to 48%, and Gettysburg College 72% to 56%.

For those students who are either turned down by their Early Decision I college, or who failed to meet the November deadline, all hope is not lost. Many colleges offer Early Decision II, with a January application deadline and notification in February – close to two months prior to the typical April 1st college response date.

New Jersey colleges that offer both Early Decision I and Early Decision II options are Stevens Institute of Technology and Drew University.

Colleges in nearby states, popular with New Jersey students, that offer both Early Decision I and II options include NYU, Syracuse University, Lehigh University, Bucknell University, Franklin and Marshall College, Gettysburg College, American University, and George Washington University.

Students who want to apply to colleges "early," but do not want to limit their options, can apply "early action" to as many colleges as they choose that offer the option. The early action application deadline is also typically November 1st, but acceptance is not binding. This means accepted students are not required to attend.

Students who hope to attend an Ivy League school should definitely consider applying under an early plan, as the competition is fierce and only a small proportion of extremely impressive applicants gain admission. Many students who hope to attend an Ivy League school don't really know the differences among these elite institutions. This becomes evident in their applications, lessening their chances of acceptance. So, any student who dreams of an Ivy League education should become well versed on the particular strengths and qualities of each of these eight remarkable institutions and then apply early to the one that's the best fit.

# The Ivy League

The "Ivy League" is a consortium of eight of the most elite colleges and universities in the United States: Harvard, Yale, Princeton, Columbia, The University of Pennsylvania, Dartmouth, Brown, and Cornell. Academically, they are all extraordinary. They are also among the wealthiest colleges and universities with endowments ranging from $51 billion at Harvard to $6.5 billion at Brown. This translates into extremely generous financial aid offers with most accepted students offered grants (scholarships) rather than loans to cover annual college costs that exceed $50,000 a year for tuition and fees (without including room and board).

All these institutions are extremely competitive in the admissions process, all brag of close to 100% graduation rates, and all have a legion of highly successful alumni. But each has its own unique qualities as well.

Harvard, the oldest university in the U.S., was founded over 385 years ago. It is one of the largest of the Ivy League schools (although only 1/3 of its students are undergrads) and hosts 41 varsity sports, which is the most of any Division I school. Its best-known and largest departments are Economics and Government, and its best-known alum include John F. Kennedy, Barack Obama and six other former U.S. presidents. Its best-known dropout is Bill Gates.

Yale attracts one of the most liberal and forward-thinking student bodies in the Ivy League and maintains a strong focus on its undergraduates. Despite its reverence for tradition, it does not have a core curriculum and there are no specific courses required for graduation. Yale alum include three recent U.S. presidents, as well as the current or former presidents of some 70 colleges and universities.

Princeton, one of the smallest of the Ivy League schools, is more conservative than Yale and a third of the size of Harvard. There is a strong focus on a liberal arts education and an emphasis on independent study with a mandatory senior thesis. It's considered one of the world's foremost research universities and is renowned for its landmark buildings designed by some of America's most well-known architects. Also, Princeton students love their eating clubs.

At Columbia University applications have doubled in recent years as its Manhattan location, in the eyes of many students, trumps every other Ivy League city. Students are also drawn to Columbia for its core curriculum, which includes the study of such classics as Homer's *Iliad* and Plato's *Republic* and determines the courses for most of a student's first two years. Proficiency in a foreign language is required, which comes in handy as Columbia offers more than 200 study abroad options.

The University of Pennsylvania (UPENN) stands out among the Ivies for its pre-professional programs, particularly in business (hosting the world-renowned Wharton School of Business), engineering and nursing. UPenn established the nation's first medical school, the first journalism curriculum, and the first psychology clinic. It embodies the foresight of its founder, Benjamin Franklin, referred to as the "ultimate visionary and pragmatist."

Dartmouth College, the smallest and most conservative member of the Ivy League, attracts outdoorsy, down-to-earth students who relish the remote, and cold, location in Hanover, NH. The college is known for its cooperative learning atmosphere where students help each other, as opposed to the cutthroat environment at some colleges where students are graded on a curve, leaving them in constant competition with their peers. Dartmouth is also known for its "D Plan" of four 10-week terms a year, allowing students to choose any three terms to attend.

Brown University, which historically was known for its student activism, does *not* emphasize grades, pre-professional programs, or sports. In fact, students are allowed to take an abundance of courses "pass/fail." Many students enjoy the option of doing group independent-study projects, taking courses that they construct primarily by themselves. Always known for its spirit of openness, Brown was the first Ivy to accept students from all religious denominations.

Although it's an easier Ivy to get into, with an early decision acceptance rate of about 27%, Cornell University is extremely competitive. It's known for an exceptionally hard-working student body, but one that also enjoys a great on-campus social life. Its Hotel Administration program is world-renowned, and its engineering and architecture programs are likewise highly impressive.

Students seeking an Ivy League education should identify the one that best matches their personality and career aspirations, as their college experience would be very different at each of these unique institutions.

Since numbers don't lie, students with dreams of attending one of the eight prestigious Ivy League colleges/universities should seriously consider applying early. Five of these schools, Brown, Columbia, Cornell, Dartmouth, and UPENN, offer an "Early Decision" plan whereby applicants sign a binding agreement that they will attend if admitted. Harvard, Princeton, and Yale universities offer a less restrictive form of early application known as "Restrictive Early Action," allowing students to also submit applications to other schools as long as none of their other applications are early action (to a private institution) or early decision.

The numbers tell the story as to why students with their heart set on attending a particular Ivy League school should seriously consider filing an early application which typically has a November

1st deadline date. All eight of these elite institutions tend to fill about half of their incoming class with Early Decision or Restrictive Early Action applicants.

Statistics indicate that the odds of getting accepted by one of these top schools increase dramatically when students sign the binding early application agreement. Brown University accepted 22% of early applicants but only 6% of regular applicants. Columbia University accepted 10% of early applicants and 3% of regular applicants. At Cornell, the gap was 27% to 9%, at Dartmouth 26% to 6%, and at Harvard University 14.5% to 4%. At Princeton, the numbers were 15.5% to 4%, at UPENN 23% to 6%, and at Yale 15% to 5%.

For students who succeed at gaining admission to one of these elite schools, the rewards are many. *U.S. News & World Report* reviewed data from *PayScale* and concluded that Ivy League graduates earn substantially more than do graduates from more than 1,500 other four-year universities. Early career median pay was reportedly $86,025 for Ivy League graduates, compared to $58,643 for graduates of other universities in 2022. That gap grew wider when considering mid-career median pay, with Ivy League graduates earning $161,888 compared to $101,777 for graduates of other institutions – a difference of more than $50,000 per year.

Not only do Ivy League students have greater potential earnings, but they typically enjoy a lower cost of education. All the Ivy League schools (with the exception of Columbia which declined to share information) are in the Top 20 on the *U.S. News Best Value Schools* list. For the most part, they have a "no loans" policy, which means they meet the full financial need of all students without requiring them to take out loans.

Ivy League students also enjoy the prestige and many benefits of attending a school with a huge endowment ($51 billion at Harvard), extremely low acceptance rate (ranging from 4% to 9%), academic excellence, and a highly accomplished faculty.

Ivy League institutions all host a powerful alumni network. At Wharton, the business school of the University of Pennsylvania, all graduates are given a prestigious Wharton email address and more than two-thirds of graduates actively engage with contacts from the alumni directory. Notable Wharton alum include Elon Musk, Donald Trump, Sundar Pichai, and Phil Murphy.

Name recognition alone often opens doors for Ivy League graduates. In addition, thcsc institutions offer their students an extensive array of professional development services, and then host powerful companies on campus that are enthusiastic to recruit these high-in-demand graduates.

What's the bar for high school students seeking admission to one of these highly competitive schools? A look at Naviance will indicate the SAT® scores of accepted students from your high school at each Ivy League institution (typically in the 1500's) as well as the average GPA (typically above 4.0 due to an abundance of AP® courses). What you can't see on Naviance is the back story: the exceptional accomplishments of accepted students, the fact that they may be a "legacy" with an alumni parent, or they may be a first-generation student to attend college, or possess other distinguishing qualities.

# Strategies for Getting "You're Accepted" Letter

Students who have their heart set on a particular college are often devastated if they do not receive a thick "acceptance letter" in the mail (or a congratulatory email) full of all the particulars for Accepted Students Day, choosing a dorm, and preparing for all aspects of life on campus.

But sometimes all is not lost. Colleges use various tactics to keep their enrollment at peak capacity and their finances in the black. The size of the student body typically diminishes as the year progresses, as some upper-class students graduate mid-year and others leave campus to pursue spring semester study abroad opportunities. So, many colleges compensate for these empty spots by offering applicants "Second-Semester Admission." Students spend what would have been their freshman fall semester in a variety of ways – studying abroad, taking classes at a local college, or even working to save money – and then move onto their college campus in time for the spring semester. The University of Maryland, Lehigh University, and the University of Southern California are among the many universities that offer some students this option. Closer to home, Fairleigh Dickinson University, in both Teaneck and Madison, N.J., promises admission to a few hundred applicants each year if they first attend, and perform well at, any community college in New Jersey.

Other colleges offer students a delayed acceptance but make them wait a bit longer to step foot on campus. An option referred to as "Guaranteed Transfer" promises students second or third year admission if they first perform well at another college. Such prestigious schools as Cornell University and Notre Dame University, as well as several colleges in the SUNY (State University of New York) system, utilize this delayed admission tool.

Of course, students should never tell a college that they are planning a temporary stay before transferring to the college of their dreams. NYU, for example, is critical of students who enroll for what is ultimately a temporary stay and admits that, in general, it would not admit a student who was not committed to a four-year undergraduate experience.

Additionally, some colleges offer "Conditional Admission" whereby a student needs to overcome a particular academic weakness before arriving on campus. Stevens Institute of Technology, for example, requires some accepted students who have not yet had calculus to take this course at their local community college in the summer before beginning their college experience. Penn State, likewise, requires certain students who are admitted to the University Park campus to first attend summer school on the campus to hone their academic skills before embarking on their freshman year. College reply letters have become a little cloudier these days – it's not always "accepted" or "denied."

Of course, the best strategy for getting "You're Accepted" letters is to submit finely honed applications. Remember, each application gets just a few minutes of attention from a college admissions officer. Sloppy or incomplete applications make a bad impression. Spelling and grammar count, as an application filled with errors indicates that either the applicant doesn't have the writing skills necessary to succeed in college, or the applicant simply doesn't care. Missing SAT® scores (when required), recommendation letters, or high school transcripts will get an application put aside and possibly not reviewed again until many fewer seats are available. Students should have one or two people carefully proofread their applications, before submitting, to check for errors and missing information. Likewise, students should be sure that all materials required from outside sources (College Board SAT® scores, teacher recommendation letters, counselor transcripts) are submitted on a timely basis.

Students should be sure that the list of colleges to which they are applying is a logical one based on their high school grades, SAT® scores, and field of interest. Information is readily available as to the average high school GPA and standardized test scores of accepted students at every college. While it's fine to have a few "reach" schools on the list, it's also important to apply to colleges where a student's high school record indicates that he/she would academically make the cut. Also, if a student indicates a career interest as an engineer, architect, or teacher, for example, it's important to verify in advance that the college offers a degree in the intended field.

Why should the college accept you? While a college will not likely ask this question so directly, it's exactly what an admissions officer is thinking while reading your application. Teens who highlight the talents, qualities, and potential they will bring to a college campus are *much* more likely to gain acceptance. There are many opportunities on a college application for students to present this information. It can be showcased on the "Activities" section of an application, enumerated on an attached resume, and written about in the application essay. Colleges are looking to populate their campus with a well-rounded student body, encompassing students with a wide range of interests, talents, and accomplishments. Be sure to let the college know how you would be an attribute to their community.

Most importantly, show demonstrated interest. As previously mentioned, colleges are well aware that most students apply to many institutions. While students are worried about getting rejected by colleges, the colleges are just as concerned about getting rejected by the students to whom they issue offers of acceptance. Therefore colleges, when evaluating an application, carefully consider the likelihood that the student, if accepted, would actually attend. Students should make every effort to visit, in person, all the colleges to which they are applying, and then personalize each application by elaborating on the qualities that make it the "perfect fit."

A New York Times *Education Life* supplement featured a cover that stated, "Admissions is unfair: Here's why." Surrounding the cynical title were clues as to the criteria that might swing a college applicant to the acceptance or rejection pile.

Before slumping into a depression, college-bound students should take comfort from the fact that 87% of colleges accept at least half of their applicants. It's the world-famous institutions that, each year, collectively reject hundreds of thousands of students who could actually thrive at their schools. This scenario plays out not only at the prestigious Ivy League colleges and universities, but also at other popular institutions. UCLA received about 140,000 applications for about 8,000 seats in last year's freshmen class resulting in an acceptance rate of less than 11%. Other universities, with acceptance rates of less than 10%, included MIT, Stanford, University of Chicago, Johns Hopkins, Duke, Northwestern, Vanderbilt, and Rice.

What college-bound students need to do, therefore, is be aware of the criteria that college admissions officers are taking under careful consideration. Some of these benchmarks are outside a student's control. Many of the top colleges favor "legacy" students with an alumni parent. Many colleges give preference to "first generation" students whose parents do not have a college education. Many colleges value geographical diversity, seeking a freshmen class that represents all 50 states and as many foreign countries as possible. According to a report by the National Association for College Admission Counseling, about half of all colleges and universities indicated that an applicant's ability to pay played a role in their admissions decision. If students can use any of these criteria to their benefit, they should highlight the information on their applications.

Of course, high school grades, the rigor of a student's course load, and SAT® or ACT® scores still carry the most weight in the admissions process. Most colleges believe that students' grades and standardized test scores are the best indicators in predicting the likelihood of their success in college.

Again, it cannot be over stressed that demonstrated interest is of key importance. Colleges do not want to get turned down by the students whom they accept as this lowers their "yield" and, ultimately, their reputation. They carefully assess the likelihood of whether a student, if accepted, would enroll. The strongest expression of demonstrated interest is for a student to apply *early decision* to a college. This assures the college that, if accepted, the student will actually enroll. Colleges also look favorably on students who interact with them in a number of ways: campus visits, contact with an admissions officer, quick response to an email.

It's important for students to go into the college application process with their eyes wide open, aware of the assets that they can use to their benefit and diligent enough to present themselves in the best possible light.

# Highlight a Talent

College-bound students with a specialized talent are in high demand by universities with a revolving student body. Almost every college hosts a gamut of sports teams, dance teams, bands/musical ensembles, and other academic and cultural organizations that require members with a particular skill. As students earn their college degree and graduate, they need to be replaced with fresh talent from the incoming student body.

High school students applying to colleges should highlight the specific skills they would contribute – and the more unique the better. Athletes who excel at less popular sports, such as lacrosse, ice hockey, volleyball, water polo, fencing, and gymnastics, have a better chance of gaining acceptance, with scholarships, than those engaged in the more common sports where there is typically an abundance of applicants.

A similar scenario exists with music. The "rarer" the instrument, the better the chance it will secure a college acceptance, often with scholarship money. College musicians in high demand are typically those proficient on the harp, oboe, tuba, bassoon, and French horn. According to campusreel.org, there are 1,534 scholarships totaling $42,500,000 available to Band/Marching Band member students.

Dancing can provide another avenue to college – especially for those with a specialty. For example, there are 31 teams registered with the Collegiate Irish Dance Association, including those at Georgetown University, UNC – Chapel Hill, University of Notre Dame/St. Mary's College, University of Michigan, Northeastern University, Ohio State University, and Villanova University. Students who excel in this genre may be able to leverage their talent to earn admission to one of these highly competitive schools.

Demonstrations of leadership experience can also make an applicant more appealing to colleges. This can be exhibited through an Eagle Scout or Gold Award project, serving as the captain of a sports team or the editor of the school newspaper, or attaining a leadership position on one's Student Council.

Participation (and hopefully leadership) on an academic club or team, such as Debate, Model UN, National Honor Society, or Girls Who Code, is also attractive to colleges who need future students who will impressively represent their school.

The key to leveraging one's activities into a college acceptance is to connect the dots for the college. Let the college know of your proficiency – whether it's in sports, music, dance, an academic field, or anything else – and how you will utilize your talent to the betterment of the college community.

# Be Aware of Online Surveillance

While most high school students maintain an active online presence, they often have no idea that colleges are monitoring their actions and "scoring" them accordingly.

The *Washington Post* reported that admissions officers at University of Wisconsin installed tracking software on their school website that indicated when a student visited their site, which pages were viewed, and how long was spent on each page. Additional information profiling the student was provided, and the student was assigned an "affinity index" estimating his/her likelihood of attending, if accepted.

University of Wisconsin is not alone. According to a report in *The Wall Street Journal*, "enrollment officers at Seton Hall University, Quinnipiac University, and Dickinson College know down to the second when prospective students opened an email from the school, how long they spent reading it and whether they clicked through to any links."

An official at Seton Hall University in N.J. acknowledged that the school assigns students a score that reflects their demonstrated interest based on 80 variables including whether they open emails from the University, how long they spend on the school's website, and how early in their high school years they started engaging with the University. Students typically have no idea that they are being tracked.

One of the largest providers of software that tracks data on prospective students is *Technolutions.* It is reportedly used by more than 1,800 colleges and universities! Its software, Slate, generates a dashboard summarizing thousands of data points on students. Schools use this information to assess demonstrated interest. While many colleges are enjoying a rising number of applicants, they are fighting to maintain or improve their yield.

Tracking students' online engagement provides solid clues as to which colleges they are most attracted to.

The National Association for College Admission Counseling surveyed some 500 schools and found that demonstrated interest is indeed important to them – on par with teacher recommendation letters and class rank – but carry less weight than a student's grades and SAT® scores.

The takeaway point for high school students is that they should research potential good-fit colleges early on, engage with them regularly, and always respond promptly to any contact initiated by the college. In short, students should assume that their online activity is indeed being tracked. By putting in the time and effort to demonstrate real interest in their colleges of choice, they will improve their "affinity index" and better their chance of ultimately getting accepted to their chosen schools.

# The Common Application

Back in 1975, administrators from fifteen colleges got together and decided to create one application that students could use to apply to any or all of the colleges within this group. This marked the birth of the *Common Application* which is now accepted by more than 1,000 colleges and universities across the United States, as well as by more than 50 international schools in 18 countries. It greatly simplifies the college application process for the millions of high school students who become immersed in it each year.

The Common App is an online application that asks a series of questions in several categories, including parents' educational history and current employment, students' SAT®/ACT®/AP® test scores and GPA, senior year courses, high school activities, and intended college major and future career.

On the "Dashboard" of the Common App, students list the colleges to which they plan to apply. The colleges all have additional questions, specific to their school, and some even require one or more supplemental essays. Once the questions are answered and essays are completed, students pay the application fee online for each college and press "submit." Students know they have successfully filed an application when confetti appears on their computer screen.

Students also provide their high school guidance counselor with a list of the colleges to which they are applying so the counselor can forward their transcripts and recommendation letters. Many high schools use the software program *Naviance* for this purpose.

The good news for New Jersey students who want to attend college in-state is that all Garden State colleges and universities, with the exception of Thomas Edison State University and Berkeley College, accept the Common App.

Schools that feature their own application, most notably state universities such as University of California, ask many of the same questions that students answer on the Common App. So, filling out the Common App is the best starting point for students in the college application process.

The Common App "goes live" on August 1$^{st}$ of each year. This means that the updated application, that will be used for the next academic year, appears online. The good news is that students can start filling out the Common App earlier than August 1$^{st}$ of the summer they are heading into their senior year, as almost all the information they input is rolled over to the new application. After August 1$^{st}$, students should read through their application and fill in any answers that did not roll over, as some questions change each year so there will likely be some questions that need to be addressed.

There's a lot of talk these days about what colleges can, and cannot, consider on students' college applications. Affirmative action has long been debated; so too has legacy preference. Students need to recognize what is in their control and what is not, and make the most of the areas in which they have full power.

On the latest Common Application there are still questions about place of birth and whether one identifies as American Indian, Alaska Native, Asian, Black or African American, Native Hawaiian or Other Pacific Islander, or White. Those who choose Asian are asked to be more specific. There's also a "school specific" question asked by most colleges to identify which applicants have family members who are alumni. How this information is used is beyond any student's control. For some, it may give their application a boost. Often, individual colleges do not download this information from the Common App.

Students do have power over the picture they paint of themselves on college applications, which are somewhat a numbers game. Colleges are impressed by students who enroll in a substantial number of AP® courses, in relation to the number that is offered at their high school. Scoring a "5" on the end-of-year exams is also notable. Colleges also pay close attention to SAT® scores, as it's the one level playing field on which they can compare all their applicants. Two million students take the SAT® exam each year and only about 300 earn a perfect 1600.

As almost all colleges seek to have a well-rounded student body, students should emphasize the qualities they will bring to the campus and neighboring community. Have they been passionate about environmental issues? Are they accomplished musicians or athletes? Have they been serving as EMT volunteers or helping the underprivileged in their community? Students can share, via the Activities section of the Common App, exactly how they have been spending their time – both in and out of school.

There is also an *Honors* section on the Common App. Its prompt reads: *Do you wish to report any honors related to your academic achievements beginning with the ninth grade or international equivalent?*

Space is allotted for up to five honors, so students should choose carefully and list them in decreasing order of importance. National awards are typically listed first, followed by state, local, and school awards.

One of the most prestigious academic honors is to be recognized as a National Merit Scholar. To be eligible, students must take the PSAT® (also known as National Merit Scholarship Qualifying Test) in 11th grade. Based on their scores, about 3% will enter the National Merit competition. Ultimately, 2/3 of these students will receive Letters of Commendation while the remaining students move on to vie for Semifinalist, Finalist, and National Merit Scholar recognition.

Another impressive academic honor is the AP® Scholar with Distinction award, which is granted to students who score a "3" or higher (and average at least 3.5) on five or more AP® exams. Students also have the opportunity of earning AP® Scholar with Honor for four AP® exams, and AP® Scholar for three exams.

Membership in the National Honors Society is also significant, as there are scholarship, leadership, service, and character requirements. Students should also note membership in any language honor society, such as the Société Honoraire de Français (French) or Sociedad Honoraria Hispánica (for Spanish or Portuguese), or if they have earned The Seal of Biliteracy.

The President's Award for Educational Excellence is another highly impressive recognition, as school principals are involved in the selection process and chosen students are awarded a certificate signed by both the President of the United States and the U.S. Secretary of Education.

Students should also note awards for high placement or participation in major academic competitions in any field, including Science Olympiad, Robotics, Model UN, Quiz Tournaments, and Geography Bee.

When deciding which five honors to include, students should consider which are highly selective, unique, relevant to one's academic interests, and/or highlights leadership potential. Any involvement that does not make the cut here can be included in the Activities section which allocates space for ten activities.

The culminating section of the Common App requires students to write an essay of 250 to 650 words. Here, too, students have the ideal opportunity to share what is important to them and why they would be an asset to the university. Often students believe their essay must be unique or entertaining. Neither is the case. It does need to be genuine and share the inner qualities of the student and what makes him/her tick. This is the perfect opportunity for students to personalize their application, sharing the qualities they would bring to the college community.

# The Essay

The acceptance of a high school senior by five Ivy League schools, as well as Stanford University, gained national attention. But it wasn't the student's stellar grades, impressive SAT® scores, or remarkable academic accomplishments that caught the world's attention. It was her Common App essay!

Brittany Stinson of Wilmington, Delaware wrote about Costco. She relayed anecdotes of her Costco visits from the time she was a two-year-old right through her teenage years. She shared her awe of the store that she labeled "the apex of consumerism" and wondered about the incomprehensible shopping habits of fellow patrons with "carts piled with frozen burritos, cheese puffs, tubs of ice cream, and weight loss supplements." She shared how the kingdom of Costco led her to "explore beyond the bounds of rational thought."

What can the millions of college-bound students learn from this story? The Costco essay personifies what college admissions officers are truly looking for in a college application essay. They want a student's personality to shine through. They want there to be a creative angle. They want honesty to seep through the essay. One of the most popular Common Application essay questions, and the one used by Brittany, states, *Some students have a background, identity, interest, or talent that is so meaningful they believe their application would be incomplete without it. If this sounds like you, then please share your story.*

This essay prompt gives students carte blanche to be creative and honest as they share their own personal story. A student might open with an anecdote, which can immediately engage the reader. This mini-story should be revealing of the student's personality and character and launch the essay into a revelation of who the student is today and what the student's vision is of the future. The very general nature of this question allows students to share a story or situation from their home life, school, work, favorite

137

activity, religious celebration, or anything at all, and describe its impact on their life and the person they are today.

The essay topic chosen by Brittany is the first of seven options offered on the Common App. Below are the other six, although students should note that while the overall topics tend to stay the same, the wording of a few essay questions may vary a bit from one year to the next.

*2. The lessons we take from obstacles we encounter can be fundamental to later success. Recount a time when you faced a challenge, setback, or failure. How did it affect you, and what did you learn from the experience?*

*3. Reflect on a time when you questioned or challenged a belief or idea. What prompted your thinking? What was the outcome?*

*4. Reflect on something that someone has done for you that has made you happy or thankful in a surprising way. How has this gratitude affected or motivated you?*

*5. Discuss an accomplishment, event, or realization that sparked a period of personal growth and a new understanding of yourself or others.*

*6. Describe a topic, idea, or concept you find so engaging that it makes you lose all track of time. Why does it captivate you? What or who do you turn to when you want to learn more?*

*7. Share an essay on any topic of your choice. It can be one you've already written, one that responds to a different prompt, or one of your own design.*

Colleges look to the essay to envision the personality of each applicant. The essay is the main opportunity for an applicant to share his/her life story, revealing human qualities that are not otherwise apparent in the application. Students should think carefully about the information they want to share with colleges that is not evident on other parts of their application, and then choose an essay topic that allows them to do so.

A great way to show demonstrated interest to each college is to personalize the end of the Common App essay. In other words, students can write one Common App essay and use the body of the essay for all of their colleges. But they should personalize the last paragraph or two to explain why they are hoping the next step of their academic journey will take place at (*fill in the name*) University.

Due to the importance of writing an interesting, grammatically correct essay, most students get help from a variety of sources. In many schools, the writing of the Common App essay is incorporated into the English IV curriculum with teachers editing their students' rough drafts. Often parents, relatives or friends offer their input as well. At times, a private counselor is hired to ensure that an impressive essay is submitted that is likely to garner the approval of college admissions officers. The end result, according to colleges, is that most of the essays they receive are good enough to be published. The problem: they seldom reflect the students' independent work.

Colleges often get a better idea of an applicant's natural writing ability and suitability for admission through the supplemental essays. Many colleges, including almost all the highly competitive institutions, require one or more supplemental essays addressing specific questions. Often the topic revolves around why the student is applying to that particular college, allowing the admissions team to assess the student's interest in, and potential match for, their institution.

Colleges also utilize the shorter supplemental questions to try to envision the personality of each applicant. Students should use this opportunity to share their human qualities that are not apparent in other parts of the application and to personalize their answers. For example, if asked, "Whom do you admire?" students should avoid the urge to write about Martin Luther King or Abraham Lincoln and instead write about a person who has impacted them in a more personal manner. If asked, "What is a book that you love?" students should skip *War and Peace* and other works of the world's most renowned authors and share a book about which they are particularly passionate or one that has influenced them in a profound manner.

Students should also utilize supplemental essays as a chance to demonstrate their interest in a particular college, and should specifically state the programs, courses, internships, study abroad opportunities, and other offerings that make the institution a perfect match for their college ambitions. Students should exercise care to ensure that these essays are well written, grammatically correct, and offer information that is not evident in other parts of their application. Just because they're not the main essay, and are not the focus of outside scrutiny by teachers and parents, doesn't mean that supplementary essays are not just as important to colleges.

# Leadership is Key Factor

It's notable when college admissions officers are all in agreement. At a gathering of high school guidance counselors, organized by the New Jersey Association for College Admission Counseling, a question was posed to a group of college admissions officers. "What quality do you most seek in the students you choose to admit?" Each admissions representative responded with the same word: Leadership.

Walk the campus of an elite university and ask any student, "What helped you get accepted to this amazing school?" You will quickly find that each student has a story to tell. It usually revolves around leadership.

Leadership takes on many forms. Some students serve as the founder, president, or other officer of a highly respected club or organization at their high school. Others are the captain of a varsity team. Still others take on leadership roles within their community. The unifying quality is that they are developing leadership skills which will impress college admissions officers and later serve their college community.

It's ideal when students gain leadership skills that simultaneously help them acquire more knowledge and experience in a field they intend to pursue in college. Future doctors can serve their communities by getting certified and working as Emergency Medical Technicians (EMTs). Future business executives can take on a leadership role with DECA, a non-profit student organization, in existence since 1946, that helps students develop financial, management, and leadership skills. If a student's high school doesn't host this club, it's the perfect opportunity to launch it!

Some students demonstrate leadership through their long-time membership in Scouts BSA (formerly referred to as Boy Scouts) or Girl Scouts. Both organizations offer a culminating project, resulting in an Eagle Award or Gold Award, providing a vast array of opportunities for scouts to exhibit their leadership skills.

Starting a project from scratch, and fully developing it with tangible results, is another distinguished form of leadership. Many unique projects were founded by student leaders who recently gained acceptance to Princeton, Harvard, and other prestigious universities.

One student launched a newsletter, *Teens Take On Medicine*, to provide high school students nationwide, who are interested in pursuing pre-med in college, with information about internships and research opportunities.

Another student started a business, *Your LockStop*, creating and selling locks with fingerprint sensors so students don't have to deal with combination locks on their lockers.

Another student initiated a YouTube channel comparing the philosophies of different religions from around the world.

The common factor is that the student was the founder, or played a leadership role, in a project that served the high school, local community, or some group in need.

# Resume Can Boost Application

The college application process begins as soon as students embark on their high school journey. Well before students identify their future college major or dream school, they start creating their personal journey through the activities, clubs, and organizations with which they engage. The best way to keep track of it all is to craft a resume and constantly update it throughout one's high school years.

A resume is a worthwhile document to have on hand, as it is often requested of high school students seeking a part time job, internship, scholarship, or inclusion in a pre-college summer program. Students should compose their initial resume during freshman year of high school, listing categories such as Academics, Athletics, Extra-curricular Activities, Volunteer Work, Employment, and any other fields in which they are engaged. Resumes should continuously be updated, with the categories posted in decreasing order of importance. Thus, the category featuring the student's most impressive accomplishments would top the resume.

On the Common Application, which is accepted by more than 1,000 colleges, students are given space to list ten activities. But they are limited in the amount of information they can include about each one. Often, students do not have sufficient space to enumerate all their accomplishments and leadership roles for each activity. Thus, a resume can fill this gap.

Many colleges provide an "upload Resume" button on the Common App, and others suggest it be included in the Additional Information section. There are some colleges that highly suggest a resume be submitted, which is very close to requiring it.

Colleges popular with New Jersey students that provide space on the Common App for a resume to be uploaded include Cornell University, Johns Hopkins University, Northeastern University,

Stevens Institute of Technology, University of Connecticut, University of Delaware, University of Pennsylvania, George Washington University, and University of North Carolina -- Chapel Hill.

By creating a resume early in their high school years, students will notice the gaps that exist while there's still time to fill them in. These may include a lack of volunteer work, leadership roles, or engagement with school and community activities.

A resume should be a continuously evolving document that students update on a regular basis. By the time senior year rolls around, it can be a valuable tool to strengthen college applications by providing impressive details of accomplishments that cannot be crammed into the limited space on the Common App. It will also be a helpful tool in applying for summer jobs, internships, and other opportunities that come along.

# Valuable Role of a Private College Advisor

For $1,500 per hour, parents can hire *Command Education* in New York City to guide their child's college application process, according to a *New York Post* article.

Fortunately, most parents seeking a private advisor for their college-bound children are not paying anything close to that figure.

Why is there such a great demand for private college consultants? It's mostly a numbers game. The American School Counselor Association (ASCA) calculates student to counselor ratios at public schools throughout the country using data from the U.S. Department of Education's National Center for Education Statistics. Its recent report showed an average student to counselor ratio in New Jersey of 337 to 1. That's better than the national average of 470 to 1, but still quite alarming. (The ASCA recommends a ratio of 250 to 1.)

High school counselors are an ideal resource for college-bound students who need guidance in a multitude of areas. For all students, details of the application process have changed greatly since the days when their parents were high school students. For those students who are either first generation college applicants or have parents who attended college abroad, the process can be even more confusing.

The problem is that high school counselors have a multitude of responsibilities for issues impacting all students in grades nine through twelve. College applications are not their sole concern. In fact, public high school counselors reportedly devote an average of 38 minutes of personalized college counseling to each student over the course of their four years. The majority of counselors' time, 77%, is spent on numerous other issues.

Private college advisors can fill the gap by guiding students and parents on all aspects of the college application process: selecting the ideal high school courses, choosing extracurricular activities that complement their academic interests, participating in volunteer work, planning when to take the SAT®, developing a list of "best fit" colleges, writing and editing impressive essays, and competently filling out college applications.

The prices for these services vary greatly. Collegebound Review, in Hillsborough, NJ, currently charges $5,995 to advise students through the entire college application process, working with them until they are accepted to the college they will attend. The company offers a complimentary consultation.

While legitimate advisors can never guarantee an acceptance to a particular college, they can certainly present students in the best possible light by personalizing their applications and emphasizing the talents and skills they will contribute to their college community.

# Study Abroad Opportunities

Almost every college and university offers students the opportunity to study abroad, as it provides an ideal experience to help them expand their horizons and become more open-minded, educated citizens of our global community. Students, in their college applications, should express an interest in studying abroad and should specify where they ideally would like to go and how they would maximize the experience. Since colleges are seeking intellectually curious students who will make the most of their opportunities, the college application is the perfect place for students to demonstrate interest by citing the specific study abroad options they find most appealing.

So where are students heading? Of the more than 300,000 students who leave North America to study abroad for academic credit each year, the two favorite locales are English-speaking: United Kingdom and Australia. These are followed, in popularity, by five European countries: France, Germany, Netherlands, Switzerland, and Spain. Asian countries popular with traveling students are South Korea, China, United Arab Emirates, Japan, and Singapore.

The University of Delaware, which launched America's first study abroad program back in 1923, offers students the opportunity to engage with more than 100 programs in some thirty countries. More than 30% of its students study abroad at least once.

Colleges with the largest percentage of students who take advantage of the opportunity to study abroad, according to *U.S. News & World Report*, include Miami University (Oxford, OH), George Washington University, Syracuse University, Boston College, University of Denver, Clemson University, American University, Stanford University, Elon University, and Villanova University.

Colleges typically charge students the same fees for international study that they would pay if they remained on their home campus, minimizing financial obstacles for those who want to experience the world.

Hundreds of thousands of college students each year recognize that the opportunity to become immersed in another culture for months at a time is something that may not happen for them again in their lifetime!

# The Art of the Interview

A Harvard University junior gained attention for being offered internships with some of the most sought-after companies: Facebook, Google, Apple, Microsoft, Goldman Sachs, and Morgan Stanley. When asked the secrets of her success, she claimed that being prepared for interview questions was very important.

To one of the most common questions, "What would you like to tell me about yourself," she offered some guidelines. She recommended that students start off with a brief introduction including their name, college, and field of study. Next, students should mention a few of their accomplishments of which they are most proud. Lastly, students should state the reasons they want to work at that particular company and share the talents and skills they possess that would be relevant for the position they are seeking. Basically, the interviewee should let the interviewer know how the company would benefit from having him/her onboard.

Students should always plan exactly what they will say when asked the most common interview questions. This is vital, whether interviewing with a prospective college or with a company for an internship or full-time job. What are some of the most frequently asked questions?

According to Glassdoor.com, a popular job and recruiting site, interviewees should be prepared to answer: What are your strengths and weaknesses? Where do you see yourself in five or ten years? What can you offer us that someone else cannot? Tell me about an accomplishment you are most proud of. Tell me about a time you made a mistake. What is your dream job?

At an interview with a college admissions officer, a student might likely be asked why they think the college is a "good fit" and what attributes they would bring to the campus. By preparing their answers well in advance and practicing their delivery skills – either in front of a mirror or to a friend or family member – students will enter their interviews feeling well prepared and confident and have the best chance of a successful outcome.

Still, almost everyone dreads the interviewing process, especially when there's a lot at stake. As previously mentioned, students should certainly practice in advance answering common questions, such as, "Why should we select you?" "What experience would you bring with you?" and "What are your proudest accomplishments?" It's easy to remember the good things we've done, and we're usually proud to talk about our assets and achievements.

Things get trickier when the interviewer asks a question such as, "Can you tell me about a time when you failed?" There is even an essay prompt on the *Common Application* that focuses on failure. It states, "The lessons we take from obstacles we encounter can be fundamental to later success. Recount a time when you faced a challenge, setback, or failure. How did it affect you, and what did you learn from the experience?"

The worse thing students can do is pretend they've never failed at anything. Is it possible for anyone to have lived through their childhood, and many of their teen years, and never have struggled in an academic subject, been cut from a sports team, lost a school election, or suffered any setback? If this is so, in the eyes of the interviewer the student might be a risky choice because no one knows how he or she will handle the inevitable setback or failure that is sure to loom in the future.

Most likely, the interviewee is simply trying to put his/her best foot forward. But it's a mistake to think that admitting to a past failure is a sign of weakness. It's actually an opportunity for a student to demonstrate that a lesson was learned, and he/she has moved on from the failure. People who think they have never failed at anything either don't have the self-awareness to recognize their weaknesses, or the self-confidence to admit to their failures.

Either way, coming off as pompous in an interview is a turn-off that is not likely to turn out well.

Another mistake interviewees sometimes make is to talk in too casual a manner and use inappropriate language when answering questions. It is never acceptable to refer, in an offensive way, to another person based on race, gender, or any other defining quality. Interviewers want to identify candidates who will represent their college in a non-biased, respectable manner.

In short, students should present themselves in the best possible light, while being honest and realistic when answering questions, even about their flaws.

# Summary of Key Strategies

Time is the greatest gift that future college-bound students can give themselves. The qualities and accomplishments that colleges are seeking in their future students are *not* ones that can be achieved in senior year of high school alone. Six strategies for acing your college applications:

1) **The earlier you start, the better.** This advice is all encompassing. You want to get great grades starting with your first semester of high school, as each grade contributes towards your overall grade point average (GPA). You should start taking the SAT® early in your high school years, as you can take the test as many times as you want and then submit just your highest scores. Practice may *not* make perfect, but the more often you take this all-important test, the more comfortable you will become with it and the more knowledgeable about the material that is covered. And it's never too early to start thinking about potential careers as it's ideal to have a chosen major when the time to fill out college applications rolls around.

2) **Recognize that colleges are looking for well-rounded student bodies, not well-rounded students.** Earlier generations of college-bound students were encouraged to become renaissance people and join many clubs, participate in sports, hold jobs, and do volunteer work. Colleges have since realized this is contrary to what they should be looking for. They don't need thousands of students who were minimally involved in a multitude of activities. Colleges now want students who have chosen a specific area of interest -- a sport, club, activity, or cause – and made a substantial impact over the course of their high school years.

3) **Do your homework.** There are more than 4,000 colleges in the U.S. alone. Many colleges are incredibly strong in a particular field of study, but just average in other academic areas. Students need to carefully research colleges to find ones that are the "best

fit" for their academic needs, while also meeting their preferences regarding geographical location, campus setting, travel abroad and internship opportunities, cost, and a host of other criteria.

4) **Demonstrate interest.** Every college is greatly concerned with its "yield" — the percent of accepted students who actually enroll. Therefore, the best strategy to gain acceptance is to convince the college/university that you will almost certainly attend if given the opportunity to do so. If possible, be sure to visit any college to which you are applying, sign in so the college has a record of your visit, and take notes of the college's specific qualities that make it so appealing. In your application essay, be sure to include a paragraph stating why that particular college is the ideal one for you.

5) **Get top grades and SAT® (or ACT®) scores.** Give colleges every reason to accept you. You are going to college for an education, and the best indicators of your strength as a student are your GPA and your standardized test scores. These are also the criteria that will be used in determining your scholarship offers, so it's wise for a multitude of reasons to put serious time and effort into earning impressive grades and scores.

6) **Recognize that optional really isn't optional.** If colleges ask for something, even if they say it's optional, do it, and do it to the best of your ability. Realize that other applicants – your competitors – will be doing everything suggested by the colleges, and you certainly don't want to be at a disadvantage.

# The End of the Road

May 1$^{st}$ is a momentous day for college-bound students. It's National College Decision Day – the deadline day for college applicants to confirm their enrollment for the upcoming fall semester.

Typically, high school seniors apply to a number of schools, spreading their applications out among perceived "stretch," "target," and "safety" schools. By April 1$^{st}$ they will have heard back from the majority of these colleges and know whether or not they have been accepted. Now, the ball is in the student's court.

Sometimes, there is a clear-cut favorite and the enrollment decision is an easy one. Other times it's a difficult choice. As May 1$^{st}$ approaches, students who are unsure of which college to choose may decide to "double deposit" – accepting admission at two schools and paying an enrollment deposit at each. While possible to do, this is considered unethical as the student will ultimately attend only one university. It's also unfair to one's peers, as it's taking up a spot that could be cherished by another student. Likewise, it's a waste of money, as enrollment deposits are typically nonrefundable.

By investing some time and resources in advance, students can make a definitive choice by the time National Decision Day rolls around. Most colleges host an Accepted Students Day where they highlight the attributes of their school and try to entice the students they have accepted to enroll. Students should make the most of this opportunity and ask any questions that are on their mind regarding the academic and social offerings at each college under consideration.

Students should also do independent research, looking into the curriculum at each school for their intended major. It's also helpful to check out the graduation rate at each college, the employment rate within six months of graduation, and the starting salary of graduates with one's intended major.

Students should investigate the campus and community life of each school under consideration. Perhaps there are favorite activities from high school that a student hopes to engage in at college, or specific new ones that will hopefully be available.

Finances also come into play in the decision of most students. It's important to know that the financial aid "package" offered by any particular college can often be negotiated. If a student's dream college offers less money than another to which the student has been accepted, there's no harm in contacting the admissions office at the preferred college and requesting that the grant money (the "scholarship" portion that does not get paid back) be reconsidered. Let the #1 college know of the other, better offers.

Usually, after doing their research and visiting each campus (one or more times), students have a good sense of which college is the "right fit" for the exciting years that lie ahead.

But sometimes, things do not go as expected or hoped for. If April 1st has rolled around and a student has not gained admission to a college of choice, all hope is not lost. The National Association for College Admission Counseling (NACAC) releases a list, in early May of each year, of colleges that still have room for students seeking admission for the upcoming fall semester. May 1st is the national response deadline for most colleges in the U.S. By that date, students must choose the college they will be attending in the fall and send in a deposit to reserve their seat (and room and board, if they are planning to live on campus). Since most students apply to a multitude of colleges, it's impossible for colleges to know for sure how many students will enroll until the reply deadline rolls around. After May 1st, colleges that have not met their target enrollment are anxious to accept additional students in order to bring in the tuition money necessary to keep on budget.

Often, even well-qualified students are not accepted to the college of their dreams. Other times, students change their minds. As the time to leave home for college approaches, students sometimes wish they had chosen a school closer to home. For these and other reasons (including procrastination), students may find themselves approaching high school graduation without a plan for the fall.

Fortunately for these students, the list that the NACAC releases each May typically includes more than 400 colleges that are still accepting applications for the upcoming fall semester. In May of 2023, for example, hundreds of colleges still had openings for both incoming freshmen and transfer students and many were still offering housing and financial aid. New Jersey schools with openings were Bloomfield College, Montclair State University, Rider University, and St. Elizabeth University. New York had 20 schools still accepting applications, including Adelphi University, Hofstra University, Ithaca College, and Pace University. Pennsylvania listed 35 schools, including Penn State University, St. Joseph's University, University of Scranton, and University of the Arts.

Of course, it is not ideal to still be applying to colleges in May of senior year. But if that's the situation, it's vital to act promptly. Students who are interested in any particular college should immediately contact its admissions department to find out exactly what materials need to be submitted. Students should also inquire about the availability of merit-based and need-based financial aid. After meeting all requirements, as quickly as possible, students should follow-up with an admissions officer and reiterate their strong desire to attend that college. Things may work out just fine after all!

# Part V. Finances, Scholarships, Avoiding College Debt

# What Students Can Do Ahead of Time

Americans aged 50 and over owe hundreds of billions of dollars in student debt for themselves and their children, according to AARP. For tens of thousands of these borrowers, their Social Security or other government payments are garnished. It shouldn't be this way. To avoid the likelihood of joining these ranks, parents and students need to do some careful planning before deciding on their college of choice.

The best scenario is for students to avoid, or at least minimize, their college debt. There are several things that students should, and should not, do to make this a reality.

While in high school, students should seek part-time jobs with companies they could continue to work for in college that offer tuition reimbursement programs. Chick-Fil-A, for example, offers its employees tuition discounts at more than 100 colleges and universities through a partnership with Scholarship America. Chipotle will pay back up to $5,250 a year in tuition costs for eligible employees. At McDonald's, restaurant crew, part-time managers, and part-time office staff, working at least 15 hours per week and in good standing, can receive up to $5,250 a year in tuition reimbursement. Starbucks will cover the full tuition for employees enrolled in Arizona State University's online program with an option of more than 100 undergraduate degrees.

While the requirements and compensation vary greatly at each, companies that currently offer some type of tuition reimbursement include Amazon, Apple, Best Buy, Comcast, Disney, FedEx, Home Depot, KFC, Papa John's, Pizza Hut, Taco Bell, T-Mobile, UPS, Verizon, and Walmart.

High school students should take their studies very seriously, as the financial cost of starting college academically unprepared can be astronomical. According to the National Assessment of Educational Progress (NAEP), which issues the Nation's Report

Card, only about a third of U.S. high school seniors are prepared for college level coursework in Math and Reading. Lack of readiness for college is a major culprit in low graduation rates, as most students who begin college in remedial courses never complete their degrees. To add insult to injury, these students frequently accumulate substantial student debt that must be paid back whether or not they ultimately graduate.

Studies have shown that anywhere from 28% to 40% of all undergraduate students enroll in at least one remedial course. This is a course they need to pay for, attend, complete assignments for, and pass, but for which they do not get any college credit. This is frustrating and expensive for students and, if several such courses are required, can considerably lengthen the number of years it takes to graduate.

Often students find that the best remedy to this dilemma is to take any necessary remedial courses at their local community college, which typically has the lowest tuition fees, while living at home. By not enrolling in a four-year college until academically ready to take courses for credit, students can greatly minimize their student debt and increase their chances of graduating "on time."

Students can usually avoid the requirement to take placement tests, which may land them in remedial courses, by earning at least the minimum SAT® scores set by individual colleges. To have the best chance of accomplishing this goal, students should take their SAT® preparation very seriously and put considerable time and energy into getting the highest scores that they can achieve. Students are allowed to take the SAT® exam as many times as they like and then, when applying to college, can send just their highest scores. Many colleges allow students to "super-score," which means the college will consider their highest Math score from one SAT® sitting and their highest Reading/Writing score from another sitting. Since most colleges award scholarship money based on SAT® scores, the easiest and most productive way for students to minimize their student debt is to maximize their

SAT® scores. Students should realize that whatever scholarship money they are awarded for their freshman year is typically renewed for the following three years as long as a minimum GPA (usually a 3.0) is maintained. So if, by earning impressive SAT® scores, a student is offered a $10,000 merit award, that would turn into $40,000 over the course of four years. The more scholarship money a student is awarded, the less debt is accrued. Once students are enrolled in college they should live simply, minimizing their expenses and using any extra money to pay down student debt before it even comes due. While it might be tempting to charge spring break to a credit card, no one wants to be paying it off, with interest, years after the memories have faded.

After graduation, when college payments start coming due, it's wise to pay off the loans with the highest interest rates first. Also, there's typically a small interest rate reduction offered to those who opt to make monthly payments via direct debit.

Some lucky students who take a job with the federal government may be eligible to have their student loans forgiven after they have been employed for ten years. Similar programs exist in some areas for teachers who work in impoverished neighborhoods.

In short, students should borrow the least amount possible and pay it off as quickly as they can. Living frugally in the short run, by minimizing expenses and borrowing the least amount possible, may allow graduates to live lavishly in the future.

# Earn College Credits Early On

Most college freshmen arrive on campus with the intention of donning their graduation cap and gown four years later. But statistics show that more than 25% of New Jersey's full-time students seeking a bachelor's degree do not reach that goal, even within six years. Regarding a four-year graduation rate, NJ.com reported it was accomplished by 51% of students at New Jersey public colleges and universities and 58% attending private institutions throughout the state.

One way for high school students to increase their chances of earning a college degree in four years (or even less) is to take college courses while still in high school, earning credits that will likely transfer to their future college. Students who are academically capable should take as many AP® (Advanced Placement) courses as possible during their high school years. The curriculum for these courses is written by The College Board, the same company that produces the SAT® exam. Students who take an AP® course, and the corresponding exam in May of the academic year, are usually given credit by their future college if they earn a test score of 4 or 5. (AP tests are scored on a scale of 1 to 5.)

AP® courses are offered in more than 30 subjects, including Art History, Music Theory, U.S. History, European History, World History, English Language & Composition, English Literature & Composition, Macroeconomics, Microeconomics, Psychology, Calculus, Statistics, Computer Science, Biology, Chemistry, Physics, Environmental Science, Spanish, French, German, Italian, Latin, Chinese and Japanese.

The *Washington Post* touted a program that utilizes AP® courses to help reign in student debt. It's called "Freshman Year for Free," and it's offered through the Modern States Education Alliance, a non-profit that helps students get through college with substantially less debt.

The way it works is that anyone -- including high school students -- can take online courses that prepare them to pass Advanced Placement (AP®) and College Level Examination Program (CLEP) tests. Students who pass eight exams can potentially earn enough college credits to bypass their freshman year and start college as sophomores -- saving 25% of tuition fees and a year of their lives!

To make this even more financially attractive, textbooks and materials are free. But there is a fee to take an AP® or CLEP exam. The College Board currently charges $97 for each AP® exam and $93 for each CLEP test. However, if cost is an issue, high school guidance counselors can often get fee waivers for needy high school students.

This is a great opportunity for students to take courses offered by professors at many of the most elite colleges and universities. The program's freshman-level courses include some taught by professors at Columbia, NYU, Rutgers, MIT, Johns Hopkins, Boston University and George Washington University.

The courses prepare students to pass AP® and CLEP exams that are accepted, for credit, by more than 2,900 universities. Students are not limited as to the number of courses they can take. The courses are self-paced, which is an asset to many students. But they should keep in mind the timing of the exams that must be passed (with certain scores) in order to earn college credits. CLEP tests can be taken year-round, but AP® exams are only offered on specific dates in May of each year.

Registration for this program is at modernstates.org. It can be quite the resume booster for a college-bound student to highlight "acing" a college level course taken with an Ivy League professor!

Another option for students, while still in high school, is to start amassing college credits by taking courses (at very affordable rates) at their local community college. Or, they can take courses online at sites such as edX.org or coursera.org where the choice of courses is almost limitless. Once in college, students can take an additional course each semester at no extra charge. This is another great way to move through college at a quicker pace and with a substantial savings of money.

When finances are a serious issue, students can also consider taking a "gap year" before beginning college. Students should apply to their colleges of choice as high school seniors and, when accepted, ask to have their admission deferred for a year. Almost all colleges are happy to oblige. Students can then work for a year, ear-marking their earnings toward their future college costs while gaining insight into the career they hope to pursue.

# Avoiding Massive College Debt

When talking about college debt, the statistics are never encouraging. In fact, the story gets sadder each year. As of 2023, more than half of all students left college in debt. For New Jersey students, the average debt was $35,202. These students joined the ranks of 44 million borrowers who collectively owe $1.75 trillion in education debt, according to statistics by *Forbes*.

The key is to avoid being a part of this grim statistic. A college education is too costly a venture for most students to enter into without a clear sense of purpose. Likewise, students should realize that there are many roads to the same destination – some much more expensive than others.

Students should avoid starting college "undecided" regarding a choice of major. There are two pitfalls here. The first is that, once a student does choose a major, many of the courses previously taken may not be part of the required course curriculum. Hence, the student will often have to spend an additional semester, year, or even longer at college. Secondly, at many colleges, students who were admitted "undecided" must apply to be admitted into their major of choice. If rejected, they can either transfer to a different college or pursue a major that may not be to their liking. The longer it takes to acquire a college degree the higher the costs add up!

Another advantage of identifying, before starting college, the academic field they wish to pursue is that students can then carefully research appropriate scholarships. Hundreds of scholarships are available to students seeking an education in STEM (Science, Technology, Engineering, Math) fields. The SMART Scholarship, for example, is offered by the Department of Defense (DOD) and provides full tuition, annual stipends, internships, and guaranteed employment to selected STEM students willing to work for the DOD upon graduation.

In addition to seeking scholarships based on their major, students should search for scholarships for any characteristics specific to them. There are scholarships for under-represented minorities, women seeking traditionally male-oriented careers, legacy students attending the alma mater of a parent, first-in-family to attend college, commitment to community service, and, of course, talent – be it in music, art, writing, athletics, or a host of other areas.

When choosing potential colleges, high school students should not necessarily reach for the stars, unless it's to a college with an impressive endowment that is generous with scholarship money. Students will find that if they apply to colleges a tier below the level of school to which they could likely get accepted, the scholarship money will almost certainly be much greater.

Another way for students to save money is to consider the cost of attending academically comparable colleges. While The College of New Jersey (TCNJ), Villanova, Drexel and St. Joseph's are all highly regarded schools in relatively close geographic proximity to each other, the cost of attending each may vary dramatically. New Jersey students get "in-state" tuition at TCNJ, which is currently $17,980. The tuition (not including room and board) at nearby schools is $61,868 at Villanova, $58,965 at Drexel and $49,610 at St. Joseph's. Of course, students should take into account that colleges may offer "merit scholarships" that greatly vary.

Students planning to major in business often seek to gain acceptance to NYU's Stern School of Business. The cost of attending this impressive college is $91,888, according to the NYU website, including tuition, food & housing, and an allotment for books & supplies, transportation, and personal expenses.

Students able to gain acceptance to NYU could reasonably expect to be welcomed at St. John's, Fordham, and Pace universities, all in NYC, as well as to a host of other institutions with impressive business schools, substantially lower costs of attendance, and generous merit money (to attract strong students) which does *not* get paid back. Parents can also negotiate financial aid offers with colleges, particularly when they have varying scholarship offers from different schools.

Students should always include an in-state public college on their list of potential schools and, if possible, consider commuting. At some four-year in-state universities, the cost of room and board is more than the cost of tuition. At Kean University, for example, the cost of in-state tuition is $12,972 while the cost of room and board is $14,834. If living at home is not an option, students should consider becoming a Resident Advisor (RA). The responsibilities include watching over the students in a particular dorm. The perks include a stipend, free room, and sometimes, free board (food)!

Students should also take advantage of work-study opportunities on campus to earn their spending money, so they won't add credit card debt to student loan debt. Part-time jobs are also a great source of income that can be directed toward college expenses. Ideally, students should seek jobs with companies that feature tuition assistance programs for part-time workers. It's motivating to get part of your tuition paid while earning a paycheck as well!

Another great way for students to save money while in college is to take advantage of the multitude of discounts available to those with a college ID. Almost every industry wants to attract college students, not just for their immediate buying power but also for their business later in life when they are earning serious incomes. Companies that focus on travel, technology, entertainment, books, cell phones, insurance, food, and many other products, often offer significant discounts to those who can flash a college ID.

By visiting the website studentadvantage.com and signing up for a card, students can save money in a vast array of industries. For example, travel discounts include up to 40% at Expedia, up to 20% on Alamo and National car rentals, and 10% on Greyhound bus fares.   Entertainment discounts include up to 40% off pre-paid tickets at AMC Theatres and up to 25% at Cinemark Cinemas. Retail discounts at greatly varying rates are offered at such popular online sites as Target.com, ChampsSports.com, and FootLocker.com.

Technology is always important to college students.   Among the companies that offer impressive savings are Amazon, Apple, Hulu, Microsoft, Spotify, and YouTube.   Students can use their devices to download The Wall Street Journal for $1 per week. Since few students are without a cell phone, it also makes good financial sense for them to check out the student discounts offered by Verizon Wireless and AT&T.

When it comes to entertainment, the very best discounts are those offered at sporting events right on campus where students pay a fraction of the price charged to the general public. For major league teams the discounts vary by city, but many offer student specials including the New York Yankees and Mets, Philadelphia Phillies, and New Jersey Devils.

Some retail stores that offer discounts to the college crowd include Nike, New Balance, Walmart, Target, Adidas, Champs Sports, J. Crew, and Vineyard Vines.

Student discounts are frequently offered at restaurants. National chains that offer student discounts include Chick-Fil-A, Dunkin', Burger King, McDonalds, Taco Bell, Dominoes, Subway, Pizza Hut, Papa John's, and Dairy Queen.   In addition, there are many regional and independent eateries near most campuses where students should ask about discounts.

The college years are an ideal time to take advantage of discounts offered by companies that are hoping to make students into life-long customers.

There are other effective financial strategies that are appropriate for specific students. Those interested in a military career can join ROTC and have some, or all, of their college costs covered in exchange for participation in ROTC on campus during their college years and a commitment to active duty afterwards.

Students who are interested in studying abroad for all of their college years will find tuition is much more affordable in Canada and the United Kingdom, where courses will still be taught in English. In the United Kingdom, undergraduate programs are typically three years long, offering another opportunity to save money.

Regardless of each student's individual circumstances and situation, the key is to think seriously about finances before heading off to college as the repercussions of educational debt can be life-changing. College graduates often find it impossible to launch independent lives – buying a home, starting a family, saving for retirement – when a large chunk of their paychecks is earmarked to repaying their college loans.

# Colleges That Meet Full Need – No Loans Required!

There are opportunities for students to graduate from college debt free, but they require some advanced research and a basic understanding of some financial aid terms. A small number of U.S. colleges have eliminated federal loans from financial aid packages, replacing them with scholarships and grants (which do not get paid back) and, sometimes, work study. The goal is to allow students to graduate debt free. But the details on eligibility vary greatly among colleges, so students need to look at the fine print.

Over the past twenty years, tuition and fees have increased dramatically at almost all colleges and universities, as indicated by statistics from *U.S. News & World Report*. Tuition and fees at private national universities have reportedly jumped 132%, those at out-of-state public national universities increased 127%, and those at in-state public national universities rose 158%.

To attract top students concerned about the financial costs of their college education, some schools are offering a "no-loans" financial aid package to all applicants regardless of financial need. But there are sometimes stipulations. Some colleges require a minimum contribution from students (expected to come from summer earnings or other sources); some have a no-loans policy only to students from certain demographics or with certain qualifications.

Princeton University, for example, instituted a no-loans policy back in 2001, but had stipulations. Starting in the 2023-24 academic year, it raised its no-loan family income cap from $65,000 to $100,000 and eliminated the required $3,500 student contribution.

Many colleges promise to meet 100% of students' financial need. What does "full need" mean? It's the difference between a family's ability to pay (based on the FAFSA and, sometimes, the CSS Profile financial aid form) and a college's cost of attendance. But colleges can meet full need in a variety of ways. Many colleges start with federal student loans and work study and then add on scholarships to reach the monetary need. Other colleges have "no-loan practices," allowing students to truly graduate debt-free.

Schools with no-loan policies for all undergraduate students, regardless of financial need, and with no minimum student contribution, include Williams College, Harvard University, and Smith College, all in Massachusetts, Swarthmore College in Pennsylvania, Bowdoin College in Maine, Davidson College in North Carolina, and Washington and Lee University in Virginia.

Some colleges that meet the full financial need of their students are "need blind," while others are "need aware." Need blind colleges offer admission to students without regard to their financial need, while need aware colleges may consider an applicant's ability to pay when deciding whether or not to offer acceptance. Students are required, on their college applications, to indicate whether they are seeking need-based financial aid.

Of course, all these colleges are highly competitive from an academic standpoint, requiring impressive GPAs and a record of accomplishments during a student's high school years. So, students who hope to benefit from the generosity and large endowments of some of these most elite institutions need to hit the ground running from the very start of their high school years.

# Best Colleges for Your Money

Americans search *Google* using the words "college" and "value" more than a million times a month, according to *Money*. The most likely reason is anxiety over the staggering cost of college. Students and parents, wanting to get the best value for their substantial investment of time and money, are smart to do some research. Studies undertaken annually by companies such as *Kiplinger* and *Money* consistently find that the best value is to attend a state university or a prestigious, well-endowed private college or university.

According to a report by *Kiplinger* on the best values among public colleges, the top-ranking schools are The University of North Carolina at Chapel Hill, University of Virginia, and University of Florida. These are followed by state universities in California, Michigan, Virginia, Wisconsin, Maryland, and Georgia. The problem is that most public universities are only a great value for families who reside in the state. For example, the tuition (without room and board) for an out-of-state student to attend UNC-Chapel Hill is $39,338, while an in-state student is billed $8,998.

When private colleges and universities are evaluated, Princeton University ranks high on everyone's list. One reason, in addition to its impressive academic credentials, is that Princeton meets 100% of each student's financial need. At Princeton, borrowing isn't part of the financial aid package; all aid is awarded in the form of scholarships and grants. No one is expected to take out loans. Of course, the catch is that very few New Jersey students are accepted to Princeton University, which admits only 4% of its applicants.

The same is true of almost all private, "best value" colleges, which include Massachusetts Institute of Technology (MIT), Stanford University, and Harvard University, each of which has an overall acceptance rate of only 4%. So, while it's great news that these elite "best value" colleges allow students to graduate virtually debt-free, the bad news is that hardly anyone can get into them.

New Jersey students seeking an affordable college education often assume that the best route is to choose an in-state public college or university. While it's a great option to consider attending one of New Jersey's eleven public colleges, it's not the only way to go.

Some of the highest ranked public universities in the country offer generous merit scholarships to lure top students from other states. At the University of South Carolina, for example, two-thirds of out-of-state freshmen receive scholarships starting at more than $9,000 a year. Top students, with high GPAs and SAT® scores over 1500, often get full-tuition scholarships.

Strong students can likewise get a great deal at Ohio State University where two thirds of out-of-state students get the $44,000 annual price tag reduced to an average cost of less than $29,000. A similar scenario exists at Miami University in Ohio where two thirds of out-of-state students get the $49,000 annual cost reduced to $35,000. Other national public universities that lower their price tag for academically impressive out-of-state students include The University of Michigan, Penn State, Iowa State and Oklahoma State universities, and the universities of Kansas and Iowa.

A handful of elite public colleges also offer need-based grants. The University of Michigan says it covers the full demonstrated financial need for out-of-state students from families earning up to $90,000.

Of course, all of these grants are competitive and are typically awarded to students in the top 25% of the applicant pool with SAT® scores over 1300.

For students who are not so anxious to spread their wings, there are plenty of great educational options at the eleven public colleges and universities in New Jersey. Rutgers is a highly ranked national university with 45,000 students and hundreds of majors at three campuses: New Brunswick, Newark, and Camden. The College of New Jersey, with a scenic campus in Ewing, ranks in the top five among regional universities in the north.

The nine other state schools, where students can frequently commute from home and eliminate expensive room and board costs, are Kean, Montclair State, New Jersey City, Rowan, Stockton, Thomas Edison State, and William Paterson universities, New Jersey Institute of Technology and Ramapo College of New Jersey.

It's no secret that attending a public university is typically the most cost-effective way to get a college degree. Furthermore, a study by *PayScale* noted that many public universities also offered the greatest likelihood of a high-paying career. Those that topped the list include Maritime Colleges, Military Academies and Technology Institutes.

One of the best public universities in the country -- based on salary potential -- is a stone's throw from Yankee Stadium, according to *PayScale* statistics. It's the SUNY (State University of New York) Maritime College in the Bronx. With an in-state annual tuition of $8,570, and an out-of-state annual tuition of $18,480, it's about as affordable as a student can hope for. Its 1,300 students can anticipate the highest median income in both early career and mid-career salaries. Part of the reason for this success is its program offerings in fields such as Naval Architecture, Electrical, Marine and Mechanical Engineering, Marine Environmental Science, Marine Transportation, and Marine Operations and Maritime Studies.

Military Academies also ranked high regarding career salary potential, which is especially impressive since tuition is free. The

United States Naval Academy at Annapolis (Maryland), The United States Military Academy at West Point (New York), and the United States Air Force Academy (Colorado) respectively topped the list, closely followed by The Virginia Military Institute.

Predictably, public universities that graduate a large percentage of STEM majors tend to have alumni with high earning potential. These students graduate with skills that are immediately in high demand. This accounts for the high national rankings of Georgia Institute of Technology, Colorado School of Mines, and the New Jersey Institute of Technology.

Other colleges that earned high honors include the University of California at Berkley, the Massachusetts Maritime Academy, and the University of California at San Diego. Students with a talent and love for math and science have some great college options.

In addition to choosing a great college that offers their major of choice, another consideration for many college-bound students is location. It's wise for students to think ahead to the city where they ultimately hope to live and work and to consider attending a college in that locale.

Top cities for job seekers, according to the career site *Indeed*, are ranked based on higher-than-average job growth rate, average annual salary, and low unemployment rate. Statistics are drawn from the Bureau of Labor Statistics. Cities currently topping the list are Atlantic City (NJ), Charleston (SC), Dallas-Fort Worth (TX), Nashville (TN), Charlotte (SC), Riverside-San Bernardino (CA), Atlanta (GA), Portland/Vancouver (OR/WA), Miami/Fort Lauderdale (FL), Portland (ME), Tampa-St. Petersburg (FL), Davenport (IA), Raleigh (NC), and Orlando (FL).

Good news for students is that the average starting pay for new college grads is historically high, hovering around $56,000, according to CNBC. Of course, the salaries that college graduates can expect is largely dependent on their field of study. Jobs in the STEM fields have starting salaries that are well above average.

Topping the pay scale are salaries for software developers, engineers, and actuaries.

Additional fields with high starting salaries are physicians in all specialties, lawyers, pharmacists, and financial managers. At the lower end of the pay spectrum for college graduates, according to CNBC, are jobs in family and consumer science, general social sciences, performing arts, social services, and anthropology. For students who have not yet chosen their path of higher education, it would be wise to take this into consideration.

If a future career in the Sun Belt is appealing, considering several of its cities topped the list for job seekers, the easiest route may be to attend a college or university in one of these warm weather cities. Students frequently convert college internships into full time jobs. College students also develop lifelong friends and potential job contacts during their college days, so it's not a bad idea to start out in a city where you would like to stay.

On the other hand, some students see their college days as an opportunity to explore the world. From a financial standpoint, there are several advantages for students to seek a college degree abroad. It's hard to beat the price tag of Europe's public universities. Statistics from educationdata.org lists annual international tuition in France as $3,400, Italy as $1,200 to $7,500, Spain as $850 to $28,000, and Germany as free to $35,000. The living expenses students can expect in these countries varies between $9,600 to $14,400. Fees for health insurance, visa, and university applications may be additional.

Prestigious universities in the United Kingdom and Australia may exceed $20,000 a year in tuition. But the fact that diplomas are typically earned in three years in the United Kingdom and for many programs in Australia still makes these international colleges a bargain by typical U.S. college price tags.

Also popular with American students, and just a short flight from many U.S. cities, is Canada. Statistics from the Canadian embassy cite more than 10,000 American students are enrolled in Canadian universities. McGill University in Montreal, referred to as Canada's Harvard, offers students the opportunity to enjoy a vibrant bi-lingual city (French/English) while getting a world-class education. And American students don't have to cross an ocean to head home for the holidays!

The "best college for your money" is, of course, a different one for each student. The key for college-bound students is to carefully consider what they are seeking in a college education, and then identify those colleges and universities that are the best match within the financial constraints that will not leave them drowning in debt once their college days are a fond memory.

# Importance of the FAFSA & Scholarship Tips

According to The College Board, about two-thirds of full-time students pay for college with the help of financial aid in the form of grants and scholarships. To be considered for most scholarships and loans, students need to file a FAFSA (Free Application for Federal Student Aid) in their senior year. It's best for families to file as soon as possible after the FAFSA is available online, which is typically on October 1st but is sometimes held until December. Some colleges have early grant deadlines, and some distribute aid on a first-come, first-served basis. As expected, the FAFSA asks questions regarding money – both on the part of the students and their parents. These questions focus on income, savings, assets, expenses, and liabilities.

The FAFSA uses financial information from a family's previous year tax returns. Most people are able to make use of a shortcut offered on the FAFSA, which is the IRS Data Retrieval Tool. As long as they've filed their previous year's tax return, they can check off that they want the FAFSA to link into it and automatically fill in the numbers on the financial questions.

A welcome characteristic of the online FAFSA is that, just a moment or two after it is submitted, it indicates a family's SAI (Student Aid Index). This is the number that is sent to all the colleges to which a student applies, letting the colleges know the amount of money the government believes the family needs to meet college expenses. Colleges then make up their financial aid offers based on this figure, typically offering students a combination of loans, grants, and work study opportunities. Until recently, the FAFSA took into account the number of children within a family that would be attending college simultaneously, but this is no longer the case.

One question on the FAFSA is whether the student would like to be approved for "work study." It's always wise for parents/students to answer "yes" to this question, as the student will then be eligible for work-related opportunities on campus. For example, if a college professor offers a student the opportunity to do paid research for him/her, the student would not be able to do so if not approved for work study. So, it's always best to leave all options open. No one will ever force a student to take on a work study job, but it's best to be able to do so if the ideal job presents itself. Work study is also a great way for students to earn spending money, as the last thing they should do is accumulate credit card debt to add to any college debt.

Filing a FAFSA as soon as possible is extremely beneficial to students in all income brackets. Many low income applicants may find that they are eligible to receive a Pell Grant which would fully cover the cost of tuition at their local community college. Other families, with students who are applying to a multitude of colleges, will be able to receive their financial aid offers in time to compare the costs and weigh their options well in advance of the May 1st deadline to accept a college offer. Getting this crucial financial information early will certainly be an aid to families about to take on, what very well may be, one of the largest expenditures of their lives.

Since the FAFSA is required by some colleges, even to qualify for merit scholarships, it's important to submit this form regardless of how high an income a family may earn.

There's also another financial aid form, the CSS Profile, that is required by about 250 colleges nationwide, including Stevens Institute of Technology in NJ, Drexel and Villanova in PA, and Fordham and NYU in New York City. It's much more intrusive than the FAFSA and asks many more financial questions. In divorce situations, both the FAFSA and CSS Profile only take into account the financial information of the parent who provides the most financial support.

In addition to filing a FAFSA, students should do everything in their power to identify, and apply for, appropriate scholarships. The best way to go through college is debt free. The fewer the loans a student takes out, the less money – with interest – a student will have to pay back. Often students are awarded scholarships in their college acceptance letters. But that's only the tip of the iceberg, as few students are offered enough money to cover tuition, fees, room and board at their college of choice. How do students cover the gap between what they are offered and what they need? The answer, too frequently, is student loans. Then, after graduation, students find themselves joining the work force in an entry-level job, with the expenses of living on their own, and with college debt that may take a decade or more to repay.

Once students know the real cost of attendance and deduct the amount they are being offered in scholarship money, they should search for as many scholarships as possible to fill in the gap.

College Board's *BigFuture* website offers a scholarship quiz to match students with 6,000 scholarships that provide $4 billion per year. By inputting one's grade level, desired degree (bachelor's), and current GPA, available scholarships are provided, along with their requirements. Students can share their desired profession, interests, affiliations, and life situations (family circumstances, illness, economic challenges, etc.) to identify best fit scholarships and their direct application links.

Discover.com offers an online scholarship search database with four million scholarships that are collectively worth over $22 billion dollars. By answering questions on ethnicity, academics, interests and activities, the system shares specific scholarships for which students may be eligible.

Another great source of information on college scholarships is one's high school guidance office where most local scholarship applications are filed. For example, scholarships are often offered by such groups as the Rotary Club, Elks, PBA, Home & School Association, Education Foundations, Women's Clubs, and both Democratic and Republican organizations. Although the awards may be on the smaller side -- between $500 and $5,000 -- the competition is limited to local, graduating students.

National scholarships, such as those offered by Discover Card, Toyota, Coca-Cola, McDonald's, Target, KFC, and Best Buy, offer scholarships that are much larger in scope, typically ranging from $10,000 to $20,000 a year. But just as the size of these scholarships is greater, so too is the competition. Tens of thousands of students nationwide seek these jackpots that are ultimately awarded to just a handful of students.

The more time and effort students devote to the scholarship search, the better the chance for success. Scholarships that require essays of over 1,000 words, or a video or other project, typically have a much smaller applicant pool. So, students shouldn't back away from those competitions that require some effort on their part.

Students should also seek scholarships from organizations with which they or their parents are personally affiliated. They might start with their church, temple, or other place of worship. If they are athletes, scouts, members of 4-H or any other particular organization, they may find that they are eligible for a scholarship. Parents, likewise, should check if their employer has scholarship money available. Families should also research scholarships for students of a particular ethnicity, as well as those for students seeking education for a particular career.

Scholly is the #1 college scholarship application in the world, as fans of the ABC-TV hit show "Shark Tank" know. It has awarded students more than $100 million dollars to date. Students can download the free mobile app in the Apple App Store or Google Play Store. Scholarship seekers are asked a series of basic questions including gender, town of residence, current grade,

grade point average, race, and college major. One can further narrow down best fit scholarships by inputting SAT® scores, extracurricular activities, and information on financial and personal situations.

According to Christopher Gray, a graduate of Drexel University who developed *Scholly* during his scholarship search, millions of dollars of available scholarship money goes unclaimed each year. College-bound students may want to seek a piece of the pie.

# ABOUT THE AUTHOR

*Susan Alaimo is the founder and director of Collegebound Review. She holds a master's degree from Columbia University and has successfully prepared thousands of students for the PSAT®, SAT®, and ACT® exams over the past 28 years.*

*Susan is an expert on the college application process and personally works with a limited number of students each year in researching best fit colleges, writing and editing creative essays, and personalizing applications to stand out to college admissions officers. She is a former college professor and high school counselor, as well as a longtime member of the New Jersey Association for College Admission Counseling.*

Visit: **CollegeboundReview.com** or Call 908-369-5362

Made in the USA
Middletown, DE
12 April 2024

52853007R00106